Founding Fathers
The shaping of America

Gerry and Janet Souter

METRO BOOKS
NEW YORK

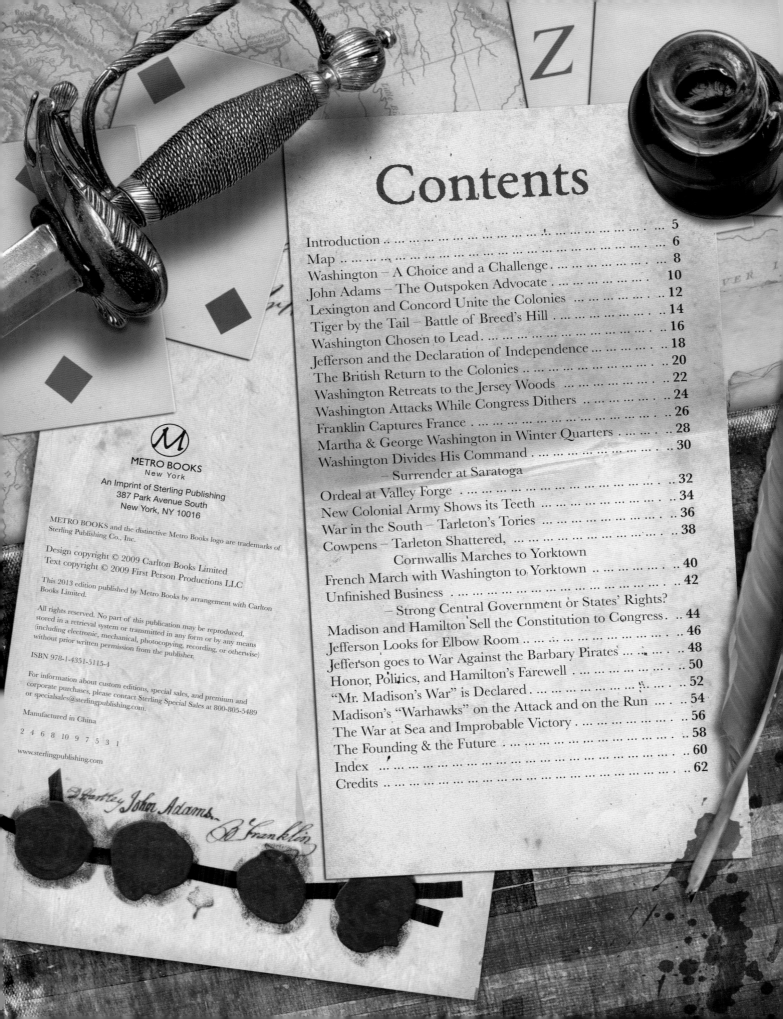

M

METRO BOOKS
New York

An Imprint of Sterling Publishing
387 Park Avenue South
New York, NY 10016

METRO BOOKS and the distinctive Metro Books logo are trademarks of
Sterling Publishing Co., Inc.

Design copyright © 2009 Carlton Books Limited
Text copyright © 2009 First Person Productions LLC

This 2013 edition published by Metro Books by arrangement with Carlton
Books Limited.

ISBN 978-1-4351-5115-4

For information about custom editions, special sales, and premium and
corporate purchases, please contact Sterling Special Sales at 800-805-5489
or specialsales@sterlingpublishing.com.

Manufactured in China

2 4 6 8 10 9 7 5 3 1

www.sterlingpublishing.com

Contents

Introduction

THEY PERSEVERED for 50 years of battle and bare-knuckle government to forge a nation. Known as the "Founding Fathers," these men, the heavy lifters and shapers of American institutions, were examples of the best of the 18th century and morally dedicated to the creation of a free country. History marks them as they arrived with the signing of the Declaration of Independence in 1776. Yet virtually none of them agreed as to what constituted a "free" country and, among flashes of brilliant intellect, they often displayed ignorant prejudices, bad taste, worse manners, naiveté, and intransigence. But over time they rose above the rubble of their disagreements and launched our great American adventure.

While many of those who signed the original Declaration of Independence and went on to agonize over the details of the Constitution, expand the boundaries westward, and establish the country's international presence achieved fame in their regional lore, six men stand out. These six stayed the course, rose from their chairs when their counsel was needed, and drove the issues that were mortised into the bedrock of our new nation.

Always the "tallest man in the room," George Washington, a peevish, quiet Virginia man driven by ambition but guided by a deeply held sense of honor, threaded his conflicted path through the worst and best days of our country's birth. Alongside him was the lawyer John Adams, an obnoxious, outspoken advocate for a somewhat imperial democracy, challenging Thomas Jefferson, the soft-spoken agrarian champion of states' rights. The Revolution brought more than independence; its dubious resolution brought virtual anarchy to the colonies. In this postwar period of confusion and consternation, a young man of equally dubious birth credentials matriculated from being Washington's wartime aide to become secretary of the Treasury: the red-headed ladies' man and brilliant pamphleteer Alexander Hamilton. Under the pseudonym "Publius," his essays helped win support for a constitution that sustained a strong central government.

Navigating through this minefield of egos and intellects came the printer-inventor-journalist-ambassador and the toast of France, Benjamin Franklin. His devotion to liberty cost him the love of his son and earned him the respect of every colonial American. The last of the six to flower was short, bald, wore black, spoke softly and literally wrote the Constitution of the United States and the first 10 amendments called the Bill of Rights. James Madison followed Thomas Jefferson into the presidency after working alongside him during the Louisiana Purchase and the Tripolitan War against the Barbary pirates. In 1812, Madison followed poor council and declared war on Great Britain, almost resulting in the United States' humiliation, but establishing its great sea power.

By the early 19th century, the six men who had never failed to answer the call to duty had departed. Washington retired to his Mount Vernon farm after giving up the presidency following two terms; Hamilton succumbed to a .50-caliber ball from Vice President Aaron Burr's dueling pistol; Franklin lived to great age and left a legacy of accomplishments. Though Madison was the last to go, it was the deaths of Adams and Jefferson on July 4, 1826, 50 years after they had taken pen in hand and risked the noose to see their country free that signaled the end of the beginning. They had never agreed upon what shape the new country should take. They had battled in the legislature, denounced each other's causes in correspondence and in print, shut themselves away in stony silence. But in the end, the wounds healed, the rhetoric faded, and once again they were two old comrades who had shared in the creation of the United States of America.

Quebec

Montreal

MAINE

Lake Superior

Lake Michigan

Lake Huron

Lake Ontario

Fort Detroit

Lake Erie

Crown Point
Fort Ticonderoga

Fort Stanwix

Saratoga

Oriskany

NEW YORK
West Point

Stony Point

Princeton

Morristown

Germantown

Trenton

PENNSYLVANIA
Valley Forge

Brandywine

Philadelphia

Lexington

Bennington

White Plains

Long Island

New York

Monmouth

Bunker Hill

Concord

NEW HAMPSHIRE

RHODE ISLAND

MASSACHUSSETTS

CONNECTICUT

NEW JERSEY

DELAWARE

MARYLAND

VIRGINIA

Richmond

Williamsburg

Yorktown

Edenton

Cahokia

Vincennes

Kaskaskia

Guilford Courthouse

NORTH CAROLINA

Kings Mountain

Charlotte

Cowpens

Camden

SOUTH CAROLINA

Augusta

Charleston

GEORGIA

Savannah

Gulf of Mexico

0   KILOMETERS   600

0   MILES   400

A
Map of

THE
REVOLUTIONARY WAR
including a
LIST OF BATTLE SITES AND CASUALTIES

THE REVOLUTIONARY WAR mirrors the societies that waged the conflict. It lasted seven years and yet relatively few key battles were fought and casualties were relatively light. Smallpox and infections killed more combatants than those killed with battlefield weapons. Washington very likely saved the revolution by insisting his troops be inoculated early on in the conflict. Another reason for the few key battles was the habit of 18th century armies to go into winter quarters and come out to fight again in the spring. Roads were terrible or non-existent and communications traveled as fast as a galloping horse. Armies and their baggage trudged along at a snail's pace, hindered by the bad quality of shoes and boots.

Light casualties despite the stand-up methods of mass firepower also reveal the gross inaccuracy of 18th century smooth-bore muskets and poor marksmanship on both sides. For the example, the "…veritable furnass…" of flanking musket fire— several thousand musket balls—that rained upon the British retreating down a narrow road from Lexington and Concord produced only 269 killed and wounded from a force of 1,800 men.

George Washington was no military genius, but he learned from his mistakes and managed to keep the army together as he retreated, feinted, and confounded the British who wanted to win big decisive set-piece battles. By the time those big conflicts came near the end of the war, the American army had been trained, blooded, toughened, and joined by their French ally. Britain had been exhausted by the preceding Seven Years War and after seven more years of fighting in the woods with colonial insurgents wanted to wash her hands of the whole business. The war ended in 1781 and thousands of brave men: American, British, French, and German had a second chance at life.

POPULATION: 3.5 million. ENROLLED SOLDIERS: 200,000. PERCENTAGE: 5.7%

TOTAL U.S. COMBAT CASUALTIES *(killed and wounded)*: **10,623**
TOTAL U.S. NON-COMBAT DEATHS *(disease, accident)*: **18,500**
TOTAL GERMAN *(Hessian)* COMBAT DEATHS: **1,200**
No reliable statistics for total British casualties

Battle	Date	Casualties
LEXINGTON-CONCORD	*April 19, 1775*	British *269* American *90*
BUNKER/BREED'S HILL	*June 17, 1775*	British *1,150* American *450*
QUEBEC	*Dec. 31, 1775*	British/Canadian *20* American *500*
WHITE PLAINS	*Oct. 28, 1776*	British *313* American *300*
LONG ISLAND	*Aug 27, 1776*	British *400* American *2,000*
TRENTON	*Dec. 26, 1776*	Hessian *974* American *4*
PRINCETON	*Jan. 7, 1777*	British *98* American *41*
BRANDYWINE	*Sept 11, 1777*	British *550* American *1,000*
FORT STANWIX	*August 3, 1777*	British *150* American *150*
SARATOGA *(3 battles)*	*Sept 19 – Oct 17,1777*	British *3,500* American *500*
GERMANTOWN	*Oct 4, 1777*	British *500* American *1,000*
MONMOUTH	*June 28, 1778*	British *350* American *300*
AUGUSTA *(KETTLE CREEK)*	*Feb 14, 1779*	British *140* American *32*
VINCENNES & KASKASKIA	*Feb 23, 1779*	British *2* American *0*
SAVANNAH	*Oct. 9, 1779*	British *57* American/French *800*
CHARLESTOWN	*May 12, 1780*	British *0* American *8*
CAMDEN	*August 16, 1780*	British *324* American *1,000*
KINGS MOUNTAIN	*Oct 7, 1780*	Tories *300* American *90*
COWPENS	*January 17, 1781*	British *100 (829 captured)* American *72*
GUILFORD COURTHOUSE	*March 15, 1781*	British *500* American *250*
YORKTOWN	*Sept 28 - Oct 19, 1781*	British *500* American *80* French *200*

Washington – A Choice and a Challenge

ABOVE General George Washington: oil on canvas painting by Rembrandt Peale in a gold frame. Washington wore this uniform of his own design throughout the French and Indian Wars.

1754

GEORGE WASHINGTON WAS born in the American colonies ruled by Great Britain on February 22, 1732 at his father's plantation on Pope's Creek near the Potomac River in Westmoreland County, Virginia. Both his parents, Augustine Washington and his mother Mary Ball Washington, were of English descent. Born and bred to the gentleman's class, George learned to supervise the slaves, exhibit expert horsemanship—he was considered one of the best horsemen in Virginia—and help with the running of the plantation. These sprawling properties were virtually self-sustaining communities, growing their own vegetables, keeping livestock, and managing water and waste as well as brewing beer or distilling their own spirits. The responsibilities were numerous and the work was hard.

When George's father died in 1743, he went to live with his half-brother, Lawrence, in Mount Vernon; Lawrence had married into the Fairfax family and was entrenched in the Virginia gentry. At age 16, George's desire to travel beyond the plantation motivated him to learn the craft of surveying and set out with transit and chains to survey the lands of Thomas, Lord Fairfax. Aged 19, after accompanying his brother to Barbados in search of a cure for Lawrence's tuberculosis, young George returned with his brother's body and eventually inherited the Mount Vernon plantation.

At the outbreak of the French and Indian War in 1754 over lands in Ohio, George signed on with the British Army as an adjutant to a military district and rose to Lieutenant Colonel of Colonial Militia. His military career, beginning in earnest at age 22, was undistinguished. His manner was brash and his bearing vain and outspoken; he had little patience and this trait led him into command difficulties during the war. After surrendering his command to the French at Great Meadows, Pennsylvania, he was paroled back to the British and sought another chance to make good. Sobered by his experiences, he volunteered to

join British General Edward Braddock and distinguished himself when Braddock's force was ambushed on the banks of the Monongahela River.

His reputation saved, Washington went on to further military success and returned in 1758 to Mount Vernon, where he vigorously expanded the estate and joined the Virginia legislative assembly, the House of Burgesses. He married a wealthy young widow, Martha Dandridge Custis, in January 1769. As his involvement with government increased, his dissatisfaction with Britain's stringent trading and taxation rules grew, as did his never-diminishing debts to the governing agents in London.

In 1774 and 1775, Washington attended the First and Second

LEFT This cartoon originally appeared in Benjamin Franklin's Gazette in 1754. It suggested that only by joining together would the united colonies survive.

King George III (1738–1820) was the grandson of George II. He only learned to read at the age of eleven. In 1760 he became king, and the next year married Charlotte of Mecklenburg-Strelitz, a German princess, who would bear him 15 children. He was a devoted family man, enjoyed gardening, and was a voluminous reader. His royal collection of 65,000 books was given to the British Museum. Although his reign did not end until his death in 1820, mental instability, diagnosed today as hereditary porphyria, effectively ended it in 1811, at which point his son, later George IV, became prince regent.

George III

Continental Congress sessions, but did not take an active part in the debates. His presence, however, being the tallest man in the room at six foot two inches and wearing a self-styled military coat and waistcoat of the Virginia militia, was undeniable.

The signing of the Treaty of Paris in 1763 formalized the new Pax Britannica map of North America. In the same year, fearing problems with the Indian tribes and the westward explorations of the colonials, King George III forbade his "loving subjects" from exploring or trading beyond the Appalachian Mountains. The Council of Three Tribes (the Ottawa, Pottawatomie, and Ojibwa) was angered over the downturn in their fortunes following the war and began destroying British forts. Citing this savagery, Britain sent 10,000 troops to Boston "for the protection of the colonies." This force represented the first step by the British Parliament toward dealing with the Indians and establishing garrisons to enforce the success of future revenue schemes. The colonists would now pay the piper.

Setting aside deep-rooted parochial differences, Massachusetts men sat with Virginians, and Rhode Islanders conversed openly with South Carolinians. They met in taverns and churches totting up their grievances and many began to think of themselves less as subjects of the Crown and more as "Americans."

MAP The Original 13 colonies following the French and Indian War and the "Proclamation line" drawn by the British beyond which the colonists could not settle. Many ignored the line.

BELOW In 1743 when George Washington was 11 years old when he inherited 10 slaves and 500 acres of land on the death of his father. As his home in Mount Vernon grew, so did the number of men, women and families needed to operate the plantation. By the time of Washington's death in 1799, 316 slaves lived on his estate.

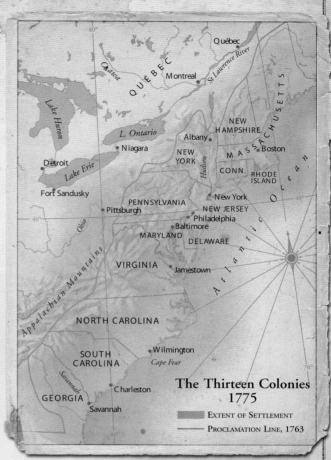

The Thirteen Colonies 1775

EXTENT OF SETTLEMENT
PROCLAMATION LINE, 1763

John Adams – The Outspoken Advocate

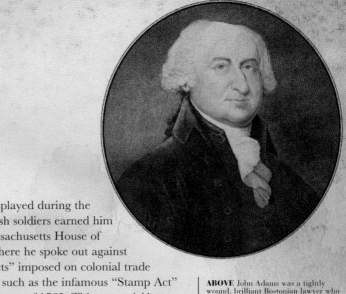

1770

As THE 13 COLONIES simmered under the roughshod handling of Parliament, Boston became a center for direct rebellion against the Crown's decrees and trade restrictions. Troops moved into the city, requisitioning quarters, and, because they were poorly paid, took jobs away from Bostonians. Fights and riots became an almost daily occurrence. Friends of the King (Loyalists or Tories) appointed to the important civil jobs mostly directed the rule of law.

On the cold night of March 5, 1770, jeering Bostonians armed with snowballs set upon a squad of harried and nervous soldiers on King Street. The taunts became slanderous. The crowd pressed closer around the squad. A flint snapped down into its powder pan and a booming shot echoed off the street stonework. A ragged clatter of shots followed and a cloud of powder smoke drifted over five civilian bodies on the cobblestones.

The soldiers were tried in a civilian court and defended by three colonial lawyers including rabble-rouser Samuel Adams's cousin, John Adams. Of the nine British soldiers tried, seven were set free, but the "Boston Massacre," as the incident became known, had been etched into the public consciousness.

Defending the soldiers was a dangerous job for Adams, a colonial lawyer who risked his reputation and his life in the eyes of the angry Bostonians, but it was in his character to take such a chance. John Adams was born in Braintree, Massachusetts (later Quincy) in 1735 to John Henry Adams and Susanna Boylston Adams. His father was a farmer but served in local politics and taught his son to read before he started school. Eventually, John matriculated to Harvard, where he studied law. After admission to the bar in 1758, he began his own climb toward national government when he became president of the Massachusetts Whigs. He married Abigail Smith on October 25, 1764.

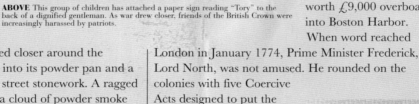

ABOVE This group of children has attached a paper sign reading "Tory" to the back of a dignified gentleman. As war drew closer, friends of the British Crown were increasingly harassed by patriots.

His courage displayed during the defense of the British soldiers earned him election to the Massachusetts House of Representatives, where he spoke out against the "Intolerable Acts" imposed on colonial trade such as the infamous "Stamp Act" of 1765. This was quickly repealed by Parliament as tax collectors feared for their lives and property.

On the night of December 16, 1773, goaded on by Samuel Adams and merchant John Hancock, a mob of 150 locals, their faces daubed with cork and with feathers in their hair, boarded the tea ships at Griffin's Wharf disguised as "Mohawk Indians," and threw 342 cases of tea worth £9,000 overboard into Boston Harbor. When word reached London in January 1774, Prime Minister Frederick, Lord North, was not amused. He rounded on the colonies with five Coercive Acts designed to put the colonies—and especially Massachusetts—in their place.

The port of Boston was closed until the cost of the spoiled tea was repaid. Massachusetts was virtually placed under direct Crown rule as its charter of 1691 was revoked and town meetings prohibited. Anti-Loyalist leaders, who were already outraged, joined together to issue invitations to the colonies to send representatives to what became the First Continental Congress. Delegates gathered at Philadelphia's Carpenter's

TEA
THE DRINK OF CHOICE

The American colonists brought their tea drinking habits with them from the Mother Country. Until they were transplanted to the North American shores, how the tea reached them was of no consequence. Since the Dutch had opened the tea trade in 1610, the British-controlled East India Company had a monopoly on English tea trade from China. Tea's caffeine was a pick-me-up and boiling the water to drink it killed bacteria. After the Boston Tea Party, however, many Americans became patriotic coffee drinkers.

Taxation no Tyranny;

AN

A N S W E R

TO THE

RESOLUTIONS AND ADDRESS

OF THE

AMERICAN CONGRESS.

Sam.ᵗ Johnson, LL.d.

LONDON:
PRINTED FOR T. CADELL, IN THE STRAND,
MDCCLXXV.

Hall on September 5, 1774. Many of the attendees had never previously strayed beyond the borders of their home colonies. Among them was delegate John Adams.

The "Suffolk Resolves," demands penned by angry Massachusetts men of Suffolk County including every possible renunciation of British Acts and edicts going back 10 years, was read to the gathering, bringing forth a hurrah. Fifty-six colonists had stood together in Congress and sent an irreversible message of defiance.

Lexington and Concord Unite the Colonies

1775

JOHN ADAMS STORMED THROUGH three years in the Continental Congress (1774–77), departing at intervals on brief leaves to recuperate from illnesses caused by nerves and overwork as well as service in the colonial legislature. His writings and widely reported pronouncements brought him fame, but his naturally suspicious and abrasive nature annoyed many of the members. As Benjamin Franklin noted, Adams was "… always an honest man, often a wise one, but sometimes, and in some things, absolutely out of his senses."

Even as members of the Congress grappled with the abstract idea of independence—only whispered at that point—they were unprepared for the fireworks that launched their cause with spilled blood.

On the night of April 18, 1775, Paul Revere was awakened and told that two lanterns burned in the steeple of Boston's Old North Church. This message signaled that British troops were being rowed to Cambridge for a raid on Lexington to capture Samuel Adams and John Hancock, and then on to Concord to seize rebel stores of gunpowder, supplies, and four brass cannon. Revere was taken to a boat and rowed to the Cambridge shore where a saddled horse awaited him. He arrived in Lexington at the parsonage of Reverend Jonas Clarke where Adams and Hancock were staying. A local man acting as a makeshift sentry complained about his shouting. Revere reportedly exclaimed, "Noise! You'll have more noise than this before long. The regulars are coming out!"

William Dawes Jr., a patriot radical from an old Boston family, joined Revere on the road at about 12.30 a.m. and they continued on to Concord. Dr. Samuel Prescott, who had been visiting a friend in Lexington, soon accompanied them in their gallop.

Following the three dusty patriots came rank on rank of Britain's best, a picked force of 700 grenadiers and light infantry commanded by Lieutenant Colonel Francis Smith of the 10th Lincolnshires and Major John Pitcairn of the Royal Marines. The soldiers had been roused from their beds after final tattoo, and packed into rowboats like sardines, and had then slogged

ABOVE This contemporary engraving from a watercolor by Amos Doolittle is a crude but accurate depiction of the brief, one-sided battle fought at Lexington between farmers, shopkeepers, and the British regulars.

THE REGULARS ARE OUT HIDE YOUR CANNON!

On April 18, 1775, Dr. Joseph Warren asked Paul Revere to ride to Lexington and warn Samuel Adams and John Hancock that British soldiers were coming for them, and that they then planned to march on to Concorde to capture hidden military stores, including four brass cannon. Two of those brass cannon were named the "Hancock" and "Adams." They were used throughout the war, and the "Adams" is at the Bunker Hill memorial today.

through knee-deep water before the long dusty march. These were men in a foul mood. However, now the word was out, and church bells began tolling on down the road.

On Lexington Green, Captain John Parker, commander of two companies of 100 local militia—the Minute Men and the Alarm Men—stood with his neighbors dressed in homespun garb, armed with hunting rifles and fowling pieces. In the gray damp of dawn, Major Pitcairn arrived and wheeled the British infantry ranks into line. He called out, "Lay down your arms you damned rebels, or you are all dead men!"

A shot rang out, followed by a high, ragged volley from the regulars. Parker dispersed his men. As they took cover, a second killing volley cut into them. British troops continued their march to Concord past the bodies of eight dead militiamen.

At Concord, the British were met by a larger body of men and fifes and drums across the green of the Muster Field. Volleys of ball and shot licked out. Gusts of gun smoke washed over the village as the militia's ranks swelled from nearby villages and the British retreated. That furnace of fire never slackened as frustrated British soldiers burned and plundered homes along the road. The exhausted expedition was relieved at Lexington by a force of over 1,000 troops from the Boston garrison. And

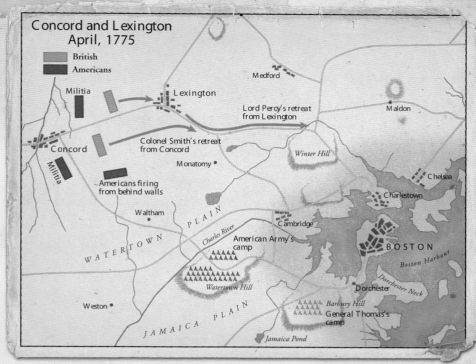

Concord and Lexington
April, 1775

- British
- Americans

Militia · Lexington · Medford · Maldon · Lord Percy's retreat from Lexington · Militia · Concord · Colonel Smith's retreat from Concord · Winter Hill · Militia · Monatomy · Chelsea · Americans firing from behind walls · Charlestown · Waltham · Charles River · Cambridge · WATERTOWN PLAIN · American Army's camp · BOSTON · Boston Harbour · Dorchester Neck · Watertown Hill · Dorchester · Weston · JAMAICA PLAIN · Barbury Hill · General Thomas's camp · Jamaica Pond

still the gunfire continued. In the wake of the retreat, powder-blackened shopkeepers, herdsmen, shoemakers, and farmers leaned on their still-warm weapons. The war of words and paper had become murderous treason and revolution.

MAP: this map shows the route from Lexington and Concorde that was followed by the British troops. Revere and his companions also followed this route.

BELOW Amos Doolittle's painting follows the Redcoats' march through Concord along a road that will be flanked by rebel fire. Major John Pitcairn and Lieutenant Colonel Francis Smith reconnoiter from a hilltop.

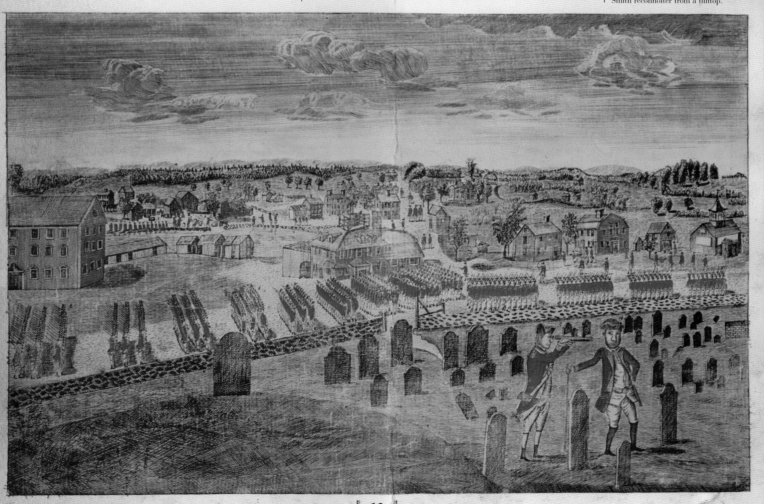

Tiger by the Tail – Battle of Breed's Hill

1775

THERE WAS NO TIME TO THINK. On May 25, major generals "Gentleman Johnny" Burgoyne, William Howe, and Henry Clinton had arrived in Boston Harbor to discover 6,000 British troops and artillery plus warships of the line circled by a shaggy mob of untrained rebels. There was no colonial army, no organization, no competent officers, no plan to defend the city against invasion. The Congress in Philadelphia might have been 10,000 miles away. If the British stormed through Boston, everything was lost. Farmers at Lexington and Concord had lit the match, but the Regulars were prepared to stamp it out. Howe, Burgoyne, and Clinton implored General Gage to secure Dorchester Heights above Charlestown, to dominate the rebels and the city. This he failed to do.

Meanwhile, the Boston Committee of Safety chose Artemas Ward, a general of militia, referred to by a fellow commander as a "fat old church warden," to thwart any British attack to break out. On June 16, Colonel William Prescott and 1,200 men towing two brass cannon hurried up Breed's Hill and began to build a redoubt of fire-step trenches, hogshead barrels filled with dirt, and bundles of wood-branch fascines completing a square with sides 132 feet long. They worked through the night.

On June 17, General Howe was amazed to discover the fortress that had sprung up overnight on the heights. He and his colleagues noted: "Never give the Yankees time to dig."

Howe's sound plan of a frontal attack and flank envelopment of Breed's Hill was delayed by six hours until his 1,500 infantry and 12 guns were in position. After 600 colonials were taken to defend Bunker Hill, grimy and game, the remaining 500 men settled in to await the British. Prescott and his officers, including Major John Stark and Captain Thomas Knowlton, had learned their trade in the French and Indian War. All their skills would be needed.

This was the pivotal fight of the war, the first face-to-face confrontation testing trained soldiers—the best in Europe—against men fighting for their homes, their families, and their lives. Those delegates in Philadelphia could only wring their hands and wonder, did the Yankee farmers, shopkeepers, frontiersmen and merchant bankers have the brass to back up the words of liberty?

After a bombardment by the Lively, Falcon, and the 64-gun ship of the line Somerset, the British attack developed. Prepared to sweep aside untutored militia, the attacking troops were surprised by the organized defense. Stark's men at the landing beach ripped through the light infantry with disciplined volley

LEFT The right flank of the British line advances to the sound of drums, muskets at the ready, eyes front. Ineffective artillery support doomed their early attacks and wasted these brave men.

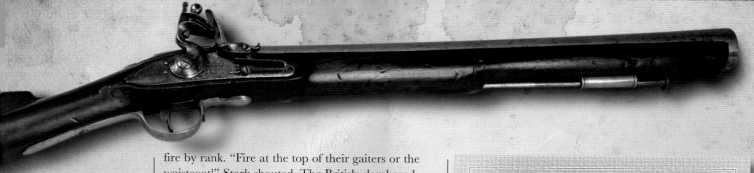

ABOVE The defenders of Breed's Hill used a variety of flintlock weapons like this short-barreled coach gun loaded with buckshot, old Spanish Fusees, fowling pieces, trade muskets, and hunting rifles.

BELOW This painting by Trumbull captures the grim attack on Breed's Hill. British regulars lean into the slope of the hill as the torrent of lead shot pours into their ranks.

fire by rank. "Fire at the top of their gaiters or the waistcoat!" Stark shouted. The British clambered up the hills into scything fire, struggling under 50 pounds of marching rations, ammunition, and accoutrements. To the rebels' rear, Charlestown had been set afire by British heated shot and exploding shot. General Ward desperately tried to gather reinforcements, while General Israel Putnam galloped from hill to hill.

Grenadiers facing up the slope toward Knowlton's fence line blazed out a platoon volley that tore though the air above the militiamen. The answering volley, aimed low, sent grenadiers tumbling, their black bearskins bouncing down the hill. At 60 yards, 30 yards, 20 yards, militia volleys decimated the British front ranks. But numbers, discipline, and clouds of grapeshot foretold the end as, after three attacks, Howe and Clinton had secured both hills by the end of the day. The butcher's bill for the 2,500 British troops was 45 percent casualties. The Americans suffered 441 casualties out of their 1,500 engaged. The Yankees had showed they had the makings of an army.

ARTILLERY FAILURE AT BREED'S HILL

Had the British been able to properly deploy their artillery at Breed's Hill, the outcome might have been different. To bombard the redoubt at the crest, ships' guns were first employed, but the 9–12 pound cannon could not be properly elevated and the target was beyond the 1,200-yard accuracy range of these weapons. Howe's artillery became mired in the marshy ground and then it was discovered the six-pounders had been provided with 12-pound shot. After horrific casualties, grape shot was finally used to carry the American redoubt.

Washington Chosen to Lead

1775

As REPORTS OF THE WORSENING situation in Boston arrived at Philadelphia, it became obvious that an "American Army" had to be fashioned from the various colonial militias. But who could lead such a force? As he sat among the delegates in his blue-and-buff militia coat, George Washington was torn. He hated being away from his beloved Mount Vernon that was in the midst of repairs. And yet his silent presence called attention to his military credentials that were known to all. He may have thought of his favorite line from the popular play Cato: " 'Tis not in mortals to command success, but we'll do more, Sempronius, we'll deserve it."

On June 14, John Adams rose to nominate "a gentleman whose skill as an officer, whose independent fortune, great talents, and universal character would command the respect of America and unite the full exertions of the colonies better than any other person alive, a gentleman of Virginia who is among us here and well known to all of us."

As Colonel Prescott led his men toward Breed's Hill on June 16, 1775, the President of Congress, John Hancock, offered the leadership of the Continental Army to the Virginia militia colonel George Washington. On accepting, the 43-year-old Washington read a prepared statement expressing doubt in his own abilities, but pledging that he would do his best: "As to pay, Sir, I beg leave to Assure the Congress that no pecuniary consideration could have tempted me to have accepted this Arduous employment … I do not wish to make any profit from it."

Barely more than two weeks later, on a rainy Sunday, July 2, 1775, General Washington rode into Cambridge to inspect his command. At his side was Major General Charles Lee, an ambitious ex-British officer. Washington traveled to each militia encampment, and as he did so men stood by their campfires and quietly doffed their wide-brimmed and tricorn hats. Officers gathered to him: Artemas Ward of Massachusetts; John Glover and his fishermen from Marblehead; the well-turned-out Rhode Islanders with their young commander, 33-year-old Nathanael Greene. There was even a portly, 25-year-old, bespectacled bookseller, Henry Knox, who seemed to have a bookworm's encyclopedic knowledge of artillery.

With these few exceptions, Washington was appalled at the motley collection of unkempt, untrained, unwashed bumpkins he had to mold into a blockading army. The British remained at anchor, making no attempt to break out. Washington wanted to put heavy artillery on Dorchester Heights quickly, because the enlistments of his "Eight-Month Army" would be up by the end of the year, and many of his troops would go home.

Born to a poor family, Henry Knox (1750–1806) quit school to apprentice as a bookbinder when his father abandoned the family. He opened his own bookstore at age 21 and began reading books on war and strategy. The rotund youth with glasses and a knowledge of guns and defenses caught Washington's attention while inspecting the militia. Soon, Knox rose to be chief of artillery. His command of guns and personal courage throughout the war eventually earned him the post of Washington's Secretary of War.

Henry Knox

British artillery was in place at the captured Fort Ticonderoga in New York. Henry Knox volunteered to take a party to bring back the guns. Leading a train of 59 iron and bronze cannons of various calibers roped to sledges and dragged by oxen, the bookseller–artilleryman made one of the great winter treks in military history. On March 4, 1776, the guns boomed above Boston for the first time.

As a result, the British garrison and anchorage were indefensible. Patriot gun muzzles

ABOVE The Grand Union was the flag of an American army that still had no name when they bottled up the British in Boston. During the Revolution, the army fought under many "American" flags.

thrust through the ports of hand-dug redoubts all along Dorchester Heights. So General Howe gathered his garrison force and many Tory families into transport ships and sailed from Boston for Halifax, Nova Scotia. On March 18, in his first victory, Washington entered the city under a new flag—the Grand Union—made of 13 red and white stripes with a Union Jack in the corner. The colonies— twice victorious—had yet to make the final break with their mother country.

TOP RIGHT Henry Knox's "noble train of artillery" and its transport over 300 miles through snow and over frozen rivers from Fort Ticonderoga to Boston was an outstanding feat of arms.

ABOVE These iron "Ice creepers" were strapped to shoes or boots allowing men to walk and hand-haul heavy loads across frozen rivers and lake beds.

Jefferson and the Declaration of Independence

1776

DURING THE SPRING OF 1776, the words "independence," "separation," and "secession" were spoken in colonial meeting houses and taverns alike. The British garrison in Boston had decamped to Halifax, and the French hinted at possible aid against England. Thomas Paine's pamphlet Common Sense stirred many colonials to consider action: "... Ye that dare oppose not only the tyranny but the tyrant, stand forth!"

Thomas Jefferson was one of them. A Virginia lawyer and member of the Continental Congress, Jefferson was a firm believer in states' rights with a small amount of authority granted to the Federal government. Born the son of wealthy landowner Peter Jefferson in 1743, he attended the College of William and Mary, began building his famed Monticello estate at the age of 26, and served in several local government offices including the House of Burgesses before being elected to the Continental Congress. In 1774 he wrote A Summary View of the Rights of British America, a guide for Virginia's delegates to the Congress, containing his view of human rights and disputing England's assertion of its power in America. "No longer persevere in sacrificing the rights of one part of the empire to the inordinate desires of another…" he wrote, addressing King George.

As support for independence grew, North Carolina, Virginia, Georgia, and the New England colonies pressed acceptance of a proposal made on June 7 by Virginia delegate Richard Henry Lee: "That these United Colonies are, and of right ought to be, free and independent states, that they are absolved from all allegiance to the British Crown…." New York abstained; Pennsylvania and South Carolina demurred; Delaware was split. As the debate continued, Congress created a committee of five to prepare a document declaring independence: John Adams of Massachusetts, Benjamin Franklin of Pennsylvania, Thomas Jefferson of Virginia, Roger Sherman of Connecticut, and the New Yorker Robert R. Livingston. The committee selected Jefferson to draft the declaration.

In a two-storey brick house at Market and 7th Street in Philadelphia, Jefferson's lodgings occupied the entire second floor. There, writing on laid paper on a portable writing desk he had designed, the Virginia planter, scientist, and inventor composed

As a child in England in the 1740s Thomas Paine (1737–1809) failed school, failed apprenticeship at his father's shop, failed in a life at sea, and failed as a tax collector for writing a pamphlet that argued for a pay raise. Fortunately, in 1774 he met Benjamin Franklin who brought him to America. Here, Paine wrote *Common Sense* and *The Crisis*, two works that greatly inspired the founders and the public during the revolution. His most famous work was *The Age of Reason* written in France (1794–96).

Thomas Paine

"We want neither inducement nor power to declare and assert a separation. It is will, alone, which is wanting, and that is growing apace under the fostering hand of our King."

Thomas Jefferson
letter to a British friend

DOCUMENTS:

1. The Virginia Resolves, created to rebut the Stamp Act of 1765, demanded that only Virginians could tax Virginians. Its strong language ignited a furor and became an early model for the Declaration of Independence.

2. Thomas Jefferson's first draft of the Declaration of Independence contains scratch-outs, marginal comments by John Adams and Benjamin Franklin and revisions that demonstrate their collaboration of ideas. The concepts are not new, but their combined application added up to treason against the Crown.

3. Following editing, additions, and subtractions by the Continental Congress to Jefferson's original document, the final Declaration was actually improved. When the final draft was agreed upon, this "engrossed" version was produced to be read out to the populace and consecrated to the ages.

(see pocket page 19)

BELOW These ink pots were used at the continental Congress in Philadelphia to sign and annotate the draft of the Declaration of Independence. Goose quills were the typical writing instrument.

his thoughts to create what he hoped would be "an expression of the American mind." By June 28, he had a "rough draft," which he shared with Adams and Franklin. After revision, Jefferson prepared a fresh draft for submission to Congress.

In Pennsylvania's soon-to-be State House, New York's delegates still awaited instructions and Delaware remained split on the resolution for independence. Meanwhile, Caesar Rodney, the third delegate from Delaware, galloped his horse through rain and lightning to cast his vote. Sodden and mud-splashed, he cast it for the resolution. New York eventually voted aye on July 19. Earlier, on July 2, 1776, Congress had approved the resolution for independence.

The next day, Jefferson, Adams, Franklin, and other members of the declaration committee presented their document. All that day Congress labored over the declaration's language—deleting its criticism of slavery—and sharpening it. On July 4, President John Hancock and Secretary Charles Thomson signed the draft, had it printed overnight, and the next morning copies were sent by post riders to the other colonies.

On July 8, in front of a crowd in the yard of Pennsylvania's Colony House, John Nixon, a member of the Committee of Safety, read the Declaration of Independence aloud. Amid the cheers and ringing bells, Loyalists and Tories booed. Jefferson's words had captured some of "the American mind," but not all. On the night of July 9, following a reading of the Declaration in New York, Patriots toppled the statue of George III, broke it up, and sent it on to Connecticut to be melted down and cast into musket balls.

The British Return to the Colonies

WHEN HE HAD OCCUPIED BOSTON on March 18, 1776, General Washington shifted five regiments of New Englanders, Virginia riflemen, Pennsylvanians, and Marylanders along with some artillery to New York. Nathanael Greene had gone ahead to scout Gravesend and the Long Island coast to map possible British landing sites. When the army arrived, they exchanged muskets for shovels and began to dig. They ringed Manhattan and its approaches with redoubts, embrasures, and trenches. Greene, Henry Knox with his big guns, and other commanders created a picture in their minds of what the British would do, and planned accordingly. Washington agreed, and so unwittingly he helped build a trap for his army. Having divided his troops and guns between Long Island and Manhattan, he left Long Island Sound, the Hudson, and East Rivers virtually undefended. This beginner's mistake gave General William Howe, his brother Admiral Sir Richard "Black Dick" Howe, and transports bearing British troops and German mercenaries a pick of landing places.

On June 29, the sun rose on 100 British sail anchored in New York's Lower Bay. Military wisdom dictated that Washington pull his divided and thinly spread army from New York and establish an inland redoubt. But Congress refused to lose face by giving up the city. Washington could have overridden their pleas, but he and his generals decided to stay and fight. American mistakes and British mastery of tactics doomed the defense even as the defenders dug deeper.

Peering across the muzzles of his guns at Old Fort George was 19-year-old Alexander Hamilton, a captain of New York artillery who had left his studies at King's College. He would rise to join Washington's staff.

ABOVE Having debarked from transport ships in New York Harbor, British and Hessian troops approach their landing point aboard rowed barges at Gravesend Bay on August 22, 1776.

While post riders carried the Declaration of Independence throughout the colonies and bells rang and patriots cheered, Congress's army floundered in confusion as it prepared for its first formal battle. Bedeviled by a hundred small details, plagued by the loss of Greene to illness, and struggling with textbook commanders, Washington's unease grew. In trying to defend too much territory with too few assets, a critical breech in the Long Island defenses at Jamaica Plain remained unguarded. Loyalist farmers pointed out the gap to British scouts.

On August 22, reefed headsails unfurled for steerageway as frigates

ABOVE This recruiting broadside – nailed up in 1776 – attempts to lure country lads into the Continental Army by showing snappily uniformed troops going through musket drill. In reality, there were few uniforms, few muskets, and sketchy drill.

General Sir William Howe (1729–1814) was commander-in-chief of the British army in America from July 1775 to May 1778. His brother, Admiral Sir Richard Howe, older by three years, commanded the British fleet along the American coast. General Howe was opposed to British coercion of North America, and Richard Howe had wanted to lead a peace delegation to the colonies after conversing with Benjamin Franklin. For both, however, duty to the Crown came first.

Howe Brothers

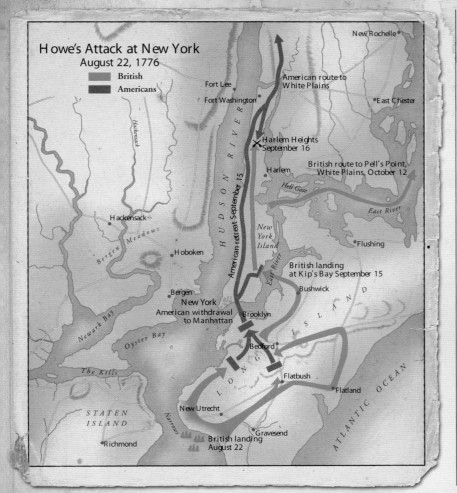

Howe's Attack at New York
August 22, 1776

- ▬ British
- ▬ Americans

New Rochelle

Fort Lee

American route to
White Plains

Fort Washington

East Chester

Hackensack

Hudson River

Harlem Heights
September 16

Harlem

British route to Pell's Point,
White Plains, October 12

Hell Gate

East River

New
York
Island

Flushing

Bergen Meadows

Hoboken

British landing
at Kip's Bay September 15

Bergen

Bushwick

New York

Brooklyn

American withdrawal
to Manhattan

East River

American retreat September 15

L O N G   I S L A N D

Newark Bay

Oyster Bay

Bedford

The Kills

Flatbush

Flatland

STATEN
ISLAND

New Utrecht

ATLANTIC OCEAN

Narrows

Richmond

Gravesend

British landing
August 22

and bomb ketches, towing 88 barges filled with the first of 15,000 British and German troops, made their way toward Long Island. Martial music from ships' bands and the skirl of bagpipes for the Black Watch troops floated over the scene. On the night of August 26, generals William Howe and Henry Clinton, and Hessian General Leopold Philipp von Heister marched with 28 pieces of artillery and regiments of foot through Jamaica Pass. They proceeded to shoot, carve, and roll up the northern flank of the startled American defenders.

They cut down riflemen—"assassins"—without quarter. Few Americans had bayonets, or knew how to use them. British artillery and sappers blew up the earthworks as the Hessians and Highlanders chopped down surrendering "peasants" and "vile enemies of the King." With Knox's heavy guns in the wrong place, the Continental Army and militias were crushed. Only evacuation could save the army, but if the British discovered such a move, surreptitious retreat would turn into rout and slaughter.

Silent line after line of Continentals disengaged from their positions on the night of August 29. Heroically, John Glover's Marblehead sailors rowed the remaining American army and its supplies from Brooklyn to safety under cover of a rainstorm and fog. The British awoke the next day to find they held a bloody but empty sack.

MAP This map shows the British landing in New York Harbor, their advance across Long Island and their driving of the Americans north, out of the city, towards White Plains, New Jersey.

RIGHT Once the British occupied New York City a fire of mysterious origins broke out. It was against British interests to burn the city that housed them. Anti-Tory arsonists were suspected.

DOCUMENT:

4. Each Continental Army soldier had to sign an oath of allegiance. The oath bound the soldier to the principals set forth in the Declaration of Independence. This copy was signed and annotated by the army's new commander, General George Washington.

(see pocket page 19)

Washington Retreats to the Jersey Woods

1776

GENERAL WASHINGTON and his amateur army had been out-thought, out-fought, and almost crushed into complete surrender. Almost. While he had the bulk of his force ready to continue the retreat toward high ground at Harlem Heights, some 4,000 remained on Manhattan near the battery commanded by Israel Putnam and Henry Knox. Able to sail with impunity, British ships shelled the city and its environs. Barges of light infantry landed alongside the enthusiastic Hessians. Neither Howe, Cornwallis, nor Clinton, who had set up a headquarters in a large house on Murray Hill, thought there was any need to rush. The shabby, untutored Americans were fleeing. Let local commanders have some sport with stragglers, rebel women and trollops, and then rest before scooping up the survivors.

General Washington was aghast and disappointed at his army's performance. His men had stood frozen, gawping at the invasion transport. Knox's artillery had fired more than 200 shots at point-blank range and did virtually no damage to the ships. Deserters were thinning his ranks as officers used the flat of their blades to slow down panic-driven flight.

Surrounded by his exhausted, beaten command, Washington felt he had to hit back if only to raise spirits. Tall, lanky Lieutenant Colonel Thomas Knowlton, who had bloodied the British nose at Breed's Hill, led a picked force of 100 Connecticut Rangers out at dawn in search of the British light infantry. They made immediate contact with 400 troops and let rip a volley. Soon, the Rangers and infantry were exchanging fire, until the honking squeal of bagpipes announced the arrival of the ranks of the Black Watch. Now outnumbered, Knowlton began a fighting retreat. Smelling blood, the light infantry surged forward, followed by the kilted Scots, blowing trumpets as if in a fox hunt and jeering as they ran.

Washington ordered 150 Massachusetts men of Nixon's brigade and some rawhide riflemen from the 3rd Virginia to strike the British infantry as it poured into an open field. In line abreast, not from behind walls, the Yankees drew up and blazed away. The light infantry and Black Watch troops stopped short. Now Greene and Putnam struck the fight and soon the British had 5,000 men embroiled. But the Americans stood their ground. With British officers and sergeants

BELOW "Hessian" soldiers, paid by the British as mercenaries during the war were recruited from many German principalities, but named after those from the principality of Hesse-Cassell.

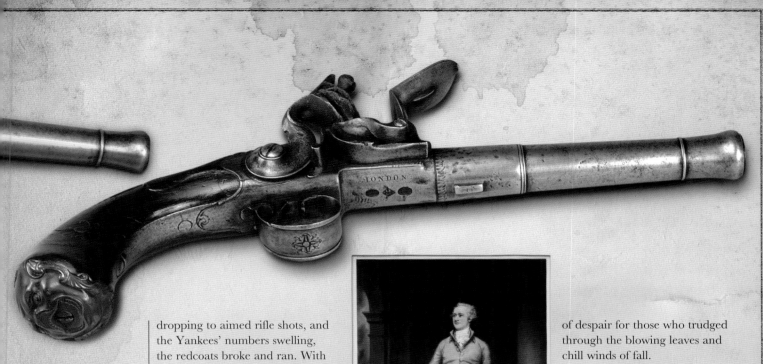

ABOVE British Officers' metal screw-barrel flintlock pistols. Barrels were threaded to unscrew at the breech to insert the ball and powder. This example was found after the battle of Breed's Hill.

BELOW The medicine chest belonging to Dr. Benjamin Rush. He kept his medicines and tools for amputation, surgery, and bleeding the patient in this collapsible chest. Refilling sometimes meant scraping bark off a tree.

dropping to aimed rifle shots, and the Yankees' numbers swelling, the redcoats broke and ran. With a "Hurrah!" the mixed lot of Americans pursued them until ordered back when British and Hessian reinforcements arrived. The victorious skirmish had restored a measure of pride to fuel the Continental Army for the long march ahead.

And a long, long march it was, as they were beaten again and again by the British pursuing them up the East River. White Plains, Kyp's Bay, Chatterton's Hill, Pell Point, the loss of Fort Washington and Fort Lee finishing the capture of Manhattan: each engagement added to the litany

ABOVE Former law student Alexander Hamilton remained with his artillery command throughout the retreat to New Jersey. Washington would later attach him to the general staff.

of despair for those who trudged through the blowing leaves and chill winds of fall.

General Charles Lee, Washington's mocking subordinate, had been taken by the British while dining in a tavern. His army was now far away and without its leader. Desertions continued as it settled in to winter camp near the west bank of the River Delaware. Howe had called off the chase until spring after establishing outposts in New Jersey to keep an eye on the dwindling American force.

As Christmas 1776 approached, Washington and his officers faced the daunting challenge of feeding, clothing, and sheltering what remained of the patriotic men and boys who had followed them into the snow-covered New Jersey woods.

WARTIME MEDICINE

During the American Revolution, illness killed more soldiers than combat. The Colonial doctor provided moral support but little else. He could set a broken leg or he could amputate it. The infection and shock of prying out a dirty lead ball with a soiled knife killed many soldiers. The doctor used herbal preparations; often the bark of the Cinchona tree (quinine). There were smallpox vaccinations, but the favorite treatment was bleeding the patient to dispose of bad "humors" in the body.

Washington Attacks While Congress Dithers

1776

HOLED UP IN PHILADELPHIA, Congress fearfully awaited the crunch of the Regulars' boots on the cobbles and a tattoo of the drums. Capture by the British meant a long drop at the end of a short rope. As December froze the ground and skinned the trees, they could only wonder. Had Washington gone completely mad?

The last of the flat-bottomed Durham boats crunched against a creaking pier at McConkey's Ferry on the east bank of the River Delaware. In the early-morning darkness of December 26, 1776, General Washington watched the last of his shivering men hustle ashore as John Glover's Marblehead sailor–soldiers exchanged their oars for muskets. Silver cakes of ice flowed past in the black water his army had just crossed. Weeks earlier, he had worked out the plan to strike the Hessian-occupied village of Trenton before dawn and already that plan was falling apart. The river crossing had taken too long. His wretched army, some with rags wrapped around their feet, would face the implacable Hessians in daylight. He mounted and trotted toward the head of the forming column, speaking to his men as he rode: "For God's sake, keep with your officers."

Washington planned to cross the Delaware at three points to surround the village and block Hessian escape routes. After traveling five miles into the teeth of a sleet storm, Nathanael Greene and Washington took the ice-slick Pennington Road, while General Sullivan continued to follow the River Road. Four artillery pieces led each column. The sky gradually lightened to a gray, snow-filled overcast as they trudged the last four miles in silence.

The Hessians had been warned of the attack, but doubted the Americans' ability. "If they attack," shrugged General Johann Gottlieb Rall, their commander, "we will give them the bayonet." That morning, while playing cards, he had received a note from a Loyalist and put it in his pocket unopened. So he missed its message: "The rebels have crossed the Delaware to attack Trenton."

At 8 a.m., Greene's men emerged from the woods and faced across a field toward warm houses filled with hot food, blankets, and the hated Hessians. Soaked and freezing, squinting into the cutting sleet, they surged forward in a rushing run called the "long trot."

"Heraus! Heraus!" cried Hessian pickets. As the Hessians tried to form up, Henry Knox bellowed "Fire!" and a round of solid shot slammed into their ranks. Hamilton's, Sullivan's, and Knox's artillery swept the stunned Germans from the main streets, while those who retreated to side streets faced hard-charging Continentals firing as they ran. General Rall tried to rally his men, but fell mortally wounded. Bridges, streets, a nearby apple orchard—all were enfiladed by American fire. Forty-five minutes after the attack began, the Hessians surrendered, leaving 21 dead in the snow, 90 wounded, and 900 as prisoners. No American had been killed in combat, and only four men were wounded.

ABOVE In a somewhat fanciful rendering, General Washington crosses the Delaware River with his troops for the dawn attack on Trenton. Hampered by the ice and sleet, the crossing took too long, forcing the daylight battle.

DOCUMENT:

5. This hand-drawn map of "Prince Town" (Princeton) shows General Washington the layout of buildings and position of British six-pounder cannon batteries. It was prepared by a patriot spy for Washington's attack on Cornwallis's rear guard following the American victory at Trenton. *(see pocket page 31)*

MAP This map shows Washington's two pronged attack on Trenton, which caught the Hessians by surprise. It was backed up by Knox's guns and militia riflemen who covered the escape routes.

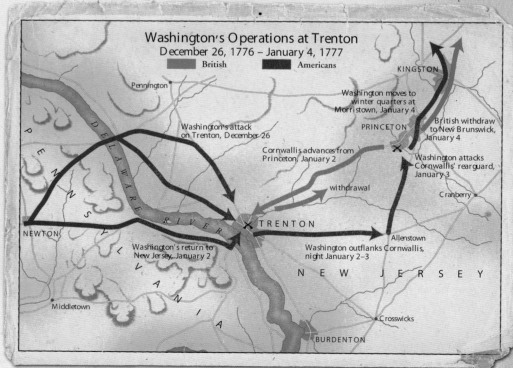

Washington's Operations at Trenton
December 26, 1776 – January 4, 1777

British | Americans

KINGSTON

Pennington

Washington moves to winter quarters at Morristown, January 4

Washington's attack on Trenton, December 26

PRINCETON

British withdraw to New Brunswick, January 4

Cornwallis advances from Princeton, January 2

Washington attacks Cornwallis' rearguard, January 3

withdrawal

Cranberry

DELAWARE RIVER

NEWTON

Washington's return to New Jersey, January 2

TRENTON

Allenstown

Washington outflanks Cornwallis, night January 2–3

P E N N S Y L V A N I A

N E W   J E R S E Y

Middletown

Crosswicks

BURDENTON

DRUMS AND MUSIC IN COMBAT

Drums and fifes were not just for morale-stirring entertainment. An officer of the day always had a drummer with him—often as young as 12 years old—to sound the call for alarm, a conference of officers or the "Tattoo." This comes from the Dutch *die den tap toe*. Taverns must turn off their "taps" so the soldiers would return to camp. During battle, drum calls were used to change marching formations, advance, retreat, or cease-fire.

RIGHT Hessian battle flags are shown to General Washington following the Trenton raid. Behind him, Hessian prisoners, still smartly dressed, look on at the rag-tag militia that had surprised and defeated them.

BELOW Washington leading his troops in the attack on Princeton made after the victory at Trenton. General Hugh Mercer died as the Americans swept over Cornwallis's rear guard.

"The troops behaved like men contending for everything that was dear and valuable," wrote Henry Knox. General Washington granted the men "who crossed the river" a cash equivalent of the spoils seized from the Hessians. Congress was ecstatic. The army savored their victory for only a day and then re-crossed the Delaware.

Shocked into action, Howe sent Cornwallis in pursuit. Again, Washington proved elusive. Decamping at night in front of Cornwallis, the Americans swung around and hit the British rearguard at Princeton. This time, Washington was in the thick of it. Men cheered as the big man with the flashing sword galloped past them, chasing the fleeing British and calling out, "It's a fine fox chase my boys!"

Franklin Captures France

1776

The oldest of the Founding Fathers and probably the most multi talented, Benjamin Franklin could be said to be the pillar of the revolutionary movement. Diplomat, publisher, statesman, author, inventor, he charmed the French while stepping delicately around the tensions that hung heavy in the European air, and brought common-sense thinking to a young country itching to fight for freedom.

Franklin spent the early days of the summer of 1776 helping to put the finishing touches on the Declaration of Independence, affixed his signature, and in late October 1776, set sail for his next mission as America's first ambassador to France. French support was vital if the colonies were to gain independence.

Franklin had established strong ties with the French years earlier, not as a diplomat, but an inventor; France was the site of his first experiments with electricity and he was a member of the French Academy of Sciences.

During the next two years, Franklin secured an alliance with the French, and obtained some loans for funding the revolution back home. He persuaded the Marquis de Lafayette to help train American soldiers, finagled guns, uniforms, and other war materiel, then set about finding merchant ships to transport the goods. He even used his powers of persuasion to form alliances with ladies of the French court.

ABOVE Benjamin Franklin signed the Declaration of Independence and was US Ambassador to France. He was largely responsible for France entering the Revolutionary War against the British and for steering General Von Steuben to George Washington to help create the Continental Army.

In turn, the French loved Franklin; his image graced snuffboxes, rings, busts. "Your father's face is as well known as the man in the moon," he wrote in a letter to his daughter.

As the war began to wind down, peace talks and negotiations took up the better part of Franklin's time in the early 1780s and, as with any final settlement, they didn't come easily. Finer points in the treaty were constantly open to debate. Finally, in September 1783, the 77-year-old Franklin signed the Treaty of Paris, granting the United States full independence. Despite several ailments, he continued to serve his country in several government posts after his return to Philadelphia. This common man capable of uncommon feats passed away quietly in 1790 at the age of 84.

Still, it was no easy task. Aware of alliances, treaties and counter-treaties which could affect support from the French, he was forced to keep a close eye on developments within the European community. Spain, England, France, and the Netherlands were in the midst of multiple squabbles, and financiers in France had to be careful about whom to support—a fledgling country an ocean away seemed to be a poor investment. Private citizens would rather lend money to their own government or neighboring countries, Franklin wrote, than "hazard it over the Atlantick." Meanwhile, officials in America pestered Franklin to obtain more loans in addition to the ones he had already secured. America was desperate. United States currency continued to sink in value, until it became useful only as wallpaper. When loans were forthcoming, Franklin kept a close eye on how the funds were spent; he insisted that monies be kept in reserve and that outstanding bills were paid first to avoid any defaults later.

He also had to deal with his fellow negotiator, John Adams, who had arrived in Paris in 1778. Adams didn't share Franklin's love for the French and thought Franklin too conciliatory in his dealings with French officials. He stated that France needed America as well; a United States victory would be to France's advantage. Some of Adams's tactless remarks to French ministers threatened to seriously undermine Franklin's mission.

What worked in Franklin's favor was his increased interest in the French way of life. He sought ways to improve conditions in prisons and asylums; hot-air ballooning caught his attention, as did papermaking. He learned the language and gave to local charities.

Martha & George Washington in Winter Quarters

1776–77

As THE WINTER OF 1776–77 closed down hostilities, the ragged and exhausted Continental Army shambled into the woods surrounding Morristown, New Jersey, and established their encampment. Except for occasional raids and skirmishes, 18th-century warfare generally took a winter time-out. The expense of maintaining an army in the field was prohibitive, considering the reduced capabilities of that force due to winter's effect on roads, fields, communications, and morale. Powder became damp in the flintlock's pan, slow matches (cotton wick soaked in lye) failed to stay alight for artillery. Paper-wrapped cartridges became sodden in their boxes. Winter was a time to rest, refit, and take stock.

General Howe retired to New York to pick up his busy social life after the shock of Trenton and Princeton. Word of those sallies failed to rock Parliament in London, which considered the capture of General Charles Lee a great coup de guerre, because he was a real commanding officer, not a jumped-up colonel of militia. The American army, it believed, was finished and could be bagged at leisure in the spring.

The land around Morristown had broad fields and plenty of timber to build 14-by-16-foot mud-caulked log huts large enough to house 12 men in each, with a fireplace. Other troops were housed in private homes, three or four to a house. With inducements of pay and heartfelt appeals, Washington had persuaded many soldiers whose enlistments were up to remain. He was also determined to maintain discipline and orderly routine in the camp. The construction of a fortification near the town was begun and required considerable labor. It was dubbed "Fort Nonsense" and while it became a supply depot, many considered it a "make-work" project.

Smallpox brought by the soldiers killed a quarter of Morristown's population. Barnyard notions of cleanliness ensured illness and contagion affected this and future winter encampments. The most common sound heard among the huts and on the parade ground was the hacking cough. Throughout the war more men would die of disease and infection than from fatal combat wounds.

At first, food was a problem. Riflemen scoured the countryside for small game, while shotgunners prowled meadows and fallow cornfields. Buoyed by the recent victories, Congress granted Washington the right to commandeer supplies as needed and camp life

improved. One day, wagons from the brig Mercury arrived, bringing supplies from Nantes, France. They carried bales of clothing, shoes, 364 cases of arms, 11,000 gunflints, and 1,000 barrels of gunpowder from the mills of Lavoisier. Thirty-four more loaded ships were gathering sail from French ports. Ben Franklin's diplomatic and commercial discussions with France were paying off.

Washington and his staff quartered in the Arnold Tavern, just off Morristown Green. The constant flow of paperwork required aides-de-camp and secretaries to have a working office space. Alexander Hamilton had joined Washington's "family" after the Princeton attack.

ABOVE The imposing Ford mansion, built 1772–74 on a hill in Morristown, was headquarters for General Washington and his staff. The elegant home was needed for visiting dignitaries and their entourages.

ABOVE Interior of a soldier's hut at Morristown, New Jersey, built from original sketches and descriptions. It held 12 men and their belongings. All meals were cooked in the hut as well.

—◆—◆—◆—

RIGHT This replica of a soldier's hut built at Morristown, New Jersey, is designed to hold two officers. Each hut had its own entrance and fireplace.

LIFE IN WASHINGTON'S MORRISTOWN HEAD QUARTERS

—◆—◆—◆—

The disparity between the crowded huts of the troops in winter camp and the general staff officers' billet at the elegant Ford home in Morristown was necessitated by the administrative needs of the army. Washington's orders had to be hand-copied by a staff of aides. Rooms were needed for conferences and housing for servants. Visiting observers from European countries brought their entourage and needed rooms. And, of course, there had to be room for the Fords and Martha Washington.

—◆—◆—◆—

Washington was fortunate to have his wife, Martha, visit, as she radiated a good cheer that uplifted the men. Later, during the winter of 1779–80, the General's staff moved into the Morristown mansion formerly owned by militia commander Colonel Jacob Ford Jr., who had died campaigning in 1777. The staff lived with the Ford family and were host to a constant visitation by foreign attachés and observers with their retinues.

The winter of 1776–77 proved the Continental Army had a strong, resourceful, and resilient core. Though it still suffered weaknesses of leadership, inexperience with military tactical execution, and a continuing disparity between regular army and unreliable militia, the army that marched into the spring of 1777 was ready to take the fight to the British once again.

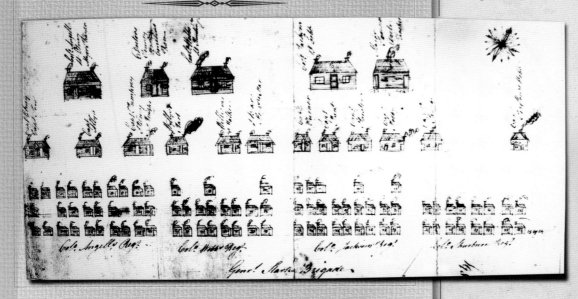

LEFT A soldier's drawing of the Morristown barracks of small wood huts laid out in company-streets. Each held 12 men with a fireplace chimney. Officer huts were higher up the hill and sheltered two officers, each with a room and fireplace—two chimneys.

Washington Divides His Command – Surrender at Saratoga

1778

CONGRESS HAD MOVED BACK into Philadelphia to continue its work on a compromise document outlining the Continental government—should the founding fathers not end up rotting in the prison hulks off Plymouth. As they debated, Washington and his staff pondered General Howe's disappearance from New York on July 23, 1777. Both Congress and Washington were aghast when Howe turned up unloading thousands of British and Hessians from frigates in Chesapeake Bay only 60 miles from Philadelphia.

Meanwhile 7,000 British, Hessians, Indians, Loyalist scouts and more than 80 pieces of artillery stepped off from Canada under the command of Major General John Burgoyne, heading south. The object—as Burgoyne understood it—was to crush Washington's army between Howe's troops and Burgoyne's expedition somewhere near Albany, New York. What to do? Washington had little choice but to send half of his army against Howe and turn over the rest to General Horatio Gates, a former British soldier in the French and Indian War. Gates preferred to delegate responsibility and was slow in decision-making. He let field commanders guide the action.

After much harassment by retreating Continentals, eventually, the British and German columns arrived at the open fields of Freeman's Farm at dawn on September 19.

British skirmishers moved forward toward the south edge of the woods 350 yards distant. They never saw the long Kentucky rifle muzzles poke out from the bushes. They heard instead what sounded like a turkey gobble. The rifles blazed and every officer among the skirmishers fell. The British returned fire at a hopeless range. After a pause, a second rifle volley ripped from the trees. Sergeants dropped and privates collapsed. The hidden riflemen, commanded by General Daniel Morgan, rushed from cover with whoops and yells. The British stood firm and produced a wall of bayonets. The riflemen turned and ran back to the woods. The battle of Freeman's Farm had begun.

Morgan's riflemen picked off cannoneers, sent gunnery officers sprawling, and riddled Burgoyne's coat and hat with holes. With battle-hardened fortitude, the British held their ground, but each day it seemed that more Yankee troops joined the fight on all sides. Up river, along Burgoyne's line of march, General John Stark cut the British river-borne supply line. Out of nowhere, Major General Benedict Arnold arrived and seemed to be everywhere, leading charges and rolling up defenses. For the besieged British and Germans to continue forward was impossible; and then General Stark sealed the road that led back north.

After 28 days of bloody combat—the Battle of Saratoga—with his men hungry and being cut to pieces by unrelenting American fire, "Gentleman

ABOVE The Battle of Freeman's Farm near Saratoga, New York, shows Benedict Arnold on the white horse leading American troops, while British General Simon Fraser is carried from the field.

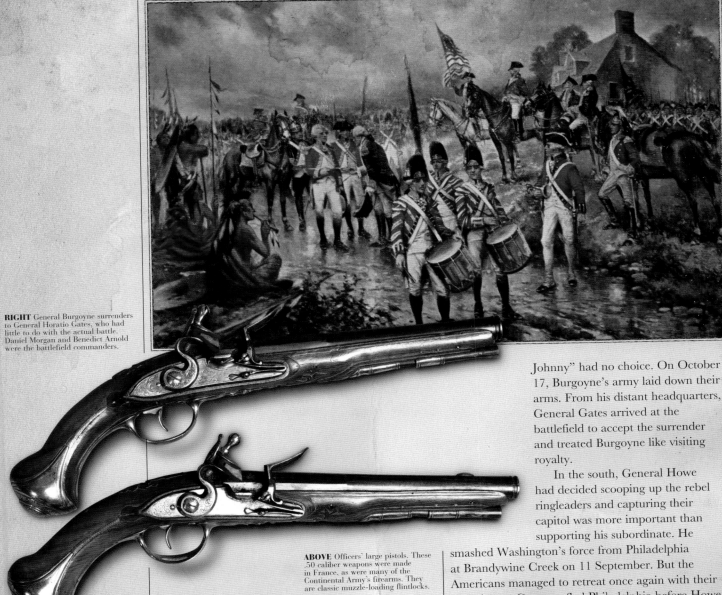

RIGHT General Burgoyne surrenders to General Horatio Gates, who had little to do with the actual battle. Daniel Morgan and Benedict Arnold were the battlefield commanders.

ABOVE Officers' large pistols. These .50 caliber weapons were made in France, as were many of the Continental Army's firearms. They are classic muzzle-loading flintlocks.

Johnny" had no choice. On October 17, Burgoyne's army laid down their arms. From his distant headquarters, General Gates arrived at the battlefield to accept the surrender and treated Burgoyne like visiting royalty.

In the south, General Howe had decided scooping up the rebel ringleaders and capturing their capitol was more important than supporting his subordinate. He smashed Washington's force from Philadelphia at Brandywine Creek on 11 September. But the Americans managed to retreat once again with their army intact. Congress fled Philadelphia before Howe moved in for the winter. This time Congress settled in the small town of York. There, the lawmakers continued work on a document they now called the Articles of Confederation. Most important, however, Burgoyne's surrender led France to shift from logistical support toward a full military and political alliance with this new United States of America. Flushed with success, Horatio Gates took his army off to Camden, South Carolina, where he was routed and fled the service to return to farming.

Brigadier General Horatio Gates (1727–1806) was an excellent administrator, but a luckless commander. He began his career as a British soldier in the French and Indian War and afterwards moved himself and family to Virginia. Washington suggested he join the militia. His ambition was fired by the victory over Burgoyne at Saratoga, but that was followed by a rout of his troops near Camden, South Carolina, in 1780. He later married a rich widow and retired to become a farmer.

General Horatio Gates

Ordeal at Valley Forge

1778

WITH THE BRITISH COMFORTABLY SETTLED into their winter quarters in Philadelphia, the ousted Continental Congress had hurried 80 miles away to the small town of York, Pennsylvania. There in the red brick courthouse in Center Square where the Declaration of Independence had been read out to the cheering populace a year earlier, the delegates continued their work on the Articles of Confederation. Feeling safe with the Susquehanna river between them and the British, they ordered a printing press, and $10,000,000 worth of currency was printed up along with broadsheets. Attempting to pay for Washington's desperately needed supplies with this money, whose inflated value swung wildly depending on the colony where it was issued or redeemed, gave rise to the slur, "Not worth a Continental."

General Washington had marched into winter quarters in Valley Forge, Pennsylvania with almost 25,000 men to house, clothe, and feed until spring. The army's engineers staked out parallel streets and drill fields, and employed soldiers to build 2,000 small log huts, each housing 12 men. Besides their quarters, they managed to build five earthen redoubts and put a sturdy bridge across the nearby Schuylkill River. But for all that, a sentry who greeted Washington one morning had to stand on his hat to keep his bare feet out of the snow.

As with Morristown the year before, Martha Washington followed her husband into camp. Her trips among the soldiers with cauldrons of hot soup and help with bachelor officers' laundry, mending, and whatever small "entertainments" were created kept morale high.

Into this frozen landscape came Marie Joseph Paul Yves Roch Gilbert du Motier, Marquis de Lafayette. He was a wealthy young Frenchman who had left his family and military career to join Washington's army without pay, in hopes of earning a command. His friendship with the General and personal bravery won him respect and a place in the hearts of all American patriots.

Another ally was a former half-pay captain in the Prussian army who had met Benjamin Franklin while the elder statesman was serving as ambassador to

ABOVE George Washington passes the colors as the troops are paraded at Valley Forge. Musters on the parade ground, guard duty, and camp routine were kept up despite the cold to keep the army together.

LEFT Winter camp life at Valley Forge was harsh. Food rations were slim and winter clothing dependent on private donations, since there was little or no money.

Von Steuben's Drill

Baron Friedrich von Steuben (1730–1794) joined Washington's command at Valley Forge, Pennsylvania, during the winter of 1778 and began training troops. He spoke no English and started small with 100 men. His musket drill broke down the process of loading and firing a musket into 15 precise steps to teach the men discipline that would be applied to his program of troop maneuvers and marching. His manual, Regulations for the Order and Discipline of the Troops of the United States, was published in 1779.

REGULATIONS
FOR THE
Order and Discipline
OF THE
TROOPS
OF THE
UNITED STATES.
PART I.

PHILADELPHIA:
Printed by STYNER and CIST, in Second-street.
M DCC LXXIX.

France. It is likely that Franklin helped him inflate his dossier to impress Congress and General Washington. So it was that Lieutenant General Baron Friedrich Wilhelm Ludolf Gerhard Augustus von Steuben arrived at Valley Forge to offer his services. He took on the task of teaching the Continental Army how to fight the British as a disciplined army, not as a mob of well-intentioned civilians.

Von Steuben spoke little English, so he started small with a squad of shivering soldiers and had Pierre Duponceau—his French secretary—and Colonel John Laurens or Lieutenant Colonel Alexander Hamilton translate his drills and commands from German into French and then into English. He slowly walked the squad through the commands of loading and firing their flintlocks, taking them through 15 steps from the musket grounded at their side to firing. He taught ranks of soldiers to wheel into line and move as a body, to master the thrust and parry of the bayonet, and to perform as a military force in the face of Europe's finest army. From squad to platoon to company, the constant drills packed down the snow on the Grand Parade Field. He and Washington, and the young Lafayette watched whole divisions dress ranks, stamp, and half-step to the rattle of drums. Von Steuben's manual of drill became part of every field officer's kit.

On the morning of May 5, 1778, startling news greeted duty officers. France had signed a Treaty of Alliance with the United States of America on February 4 committing troops and ships to the war. They were no longer alone.

RIGHT Washington and Lafayette at Valley Forge. The Marquis de Lafayette came from France and volunteered to fight with Washington. They remained lifelong friends and Lafayette fought significant battles in 1780–81. He became an American hero.

New Colonial Army Shows its Teeth

1778

As the concerted efforts of Benjamin Franklin and, for a time, John Adams won military aid and the bankroll of France for the revolution, their strategic coup had a pronounced tactical result in the colonies. Sir Henry Clinton had just ensconced himself in Philadelphia as Howe's replacement, commanding all British forces in North America, when he received orders from London to ship 5,000 of his troops to the West Indies to fight the French. He had to transport another 3,000 troops to St. Augustine, Florida, to guard against Spain's probable entry into the war. What remained of the Philadelphia occupation force was ordered to New York. The colonial contest had become a part of the larger war with France.

British Loyalists had flocked to Philadelphia once the British had taken it. Now they would be abandoned to the rebels' wrath. Clinton also feared the appearance of French warships, and so decided to send the Loyalists by water routes to British-occupied territory around New York, while he marched his troops overland, crossing the River Delaware into New Jersey on June 18, 1778.

By June 1, Clinton's evacuation plan was in Washington's hands. He gave the opportunity to attack Clinton's troops and supply train to General Charles Lee, who immediately turned it down and used every opportunity to slander Washington's leadership and character. Lee was convinced American troops were no match for the British. When the army of 6,000 men was then given to Lafayette and the size of the committed force became known, Lee immediately reconsidered and demanded the command. Obeying protocol, Washington acceded and Lee rode off to seize control.

Though Daniel Morgan shadowed the British, opportunity after opportunity was lost to launch an attack. Lafayette and Anthony Wayne seethed as they listened to British wagons rumble along a road near Monmouth Courthouse. Finally, word reached Washington, who ordered Lee to attack immediately. Lee threw up his hands and on June 28 scattered his men all along the British line of march. The result was uncoordinated chaos. Yet the troops trained by von Steuben proved better than their commander.

ABOVE General George Washington confronts General Charles Lee at Monmouth and relieves him of command for retreating. Washington went on to lead the troops back against the British and saved the army once more.

Benedict Arnold

Benedict Arnold (1741–1801) was an American officer of great personal bravery matched only by his ambition. A man of action and great appetites, he was badly wounded in the leg and blamed Congress for overlooking his claims for advancement. He gave plans of West Point's defense to Loyalist spy John André who was caught and hanged. Arnold fled the United States and led troops against the Americans. He died a pauper in England and was buried in his Continental uniform.

Anthony Wayne's infantry were hotly engaged when elite British cavalry, the Queen's Rangers and 16th Dragoons, thundered forward. Earlier, a cavalry charge had always driven the American rabble to flee. Now, the Continentals wheeled into double lines and delivered crashing volleys that emptied British saddles. "Fix bayonets!" rolled down the line and the Americans advanced, driving the Rangers and Dragoons back upon their own infantry.

At this point, Lee abandoned Wayne, Lafayette, Morgan, and the rest and, pounding to the rear, called for a full retreat. Lafayette, his sword bloodied, his men fighting toe to toe with the British, looked around to see a solitary figure riding toward him on a white horse. Dusty, streaked with sweat, and cantering with his cocked hat held high, George Washington's "presence stopped the retreat," wrote the Marquis. The Americans rallied and held, but could not advance. The magnificently disciplined British had been fighting this kind of battle for 100 years. Aided by darkness, the British wagon train proceeded toward the ships waiting at Sandy Hook.

Washington sent Lee to the rear to await the court martial that would end his career. The Battle of Monmouth ended in a draw, but the Americans had fought on British terms and broken the scarlet line. The main armies would never face each other again bayonet to bayonet because the war moved south into other commands. But on the night of June 28, both George Washington and the Marquis de Lafayette fell asleep beneath a gnarled old tree on soil won by the first United States Army.

RIGHT This tricorn hat was called a "cocked hat" because it carries a colored ribbon or "cockade" in its brim. This particular hat belonged to a non-commissioned officer, a corporal, or sergeant. When uniforms were few, colored ribbon became the only telltale for rank.

BELOW Major John André, a British spy, is captured with the plans to the Hudson River defenses in his boot. His collaboration with American hero General Benedict Arnold rocked the army and General Washington.

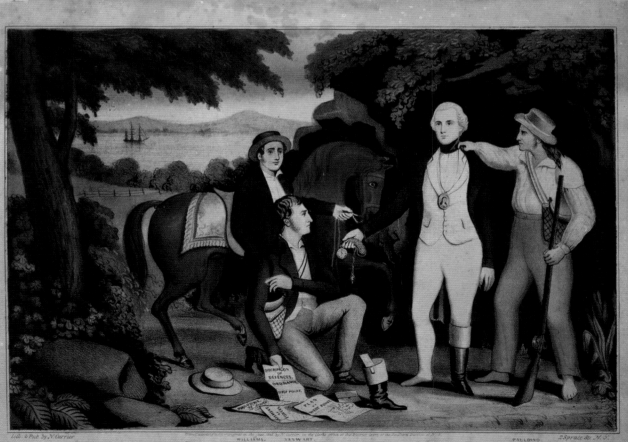

CAPTURE OF ANDRE 1780.

War in the South – Tarleton's Tories

1779

In 1779, Sir Henry Clinton decided an adventure in the south would be good for his army regulars and would allow him to exercise his scheme for using thousands of Tories who, he believed, would flock to the Union Jack. He also commanded Lieutenant Colonel Banastre Tarleton, the ruthless leader of "Tarleton's Tory Legion," a bloodthirsty cavalry troop known for scourging rebel civilians as well as enemy troops. Cutting down surrendering soldiers and begging civilians alike was dubbed "Tarleton's Quarter."

With Washington tied down in front of New York, fighting in the south was left to a mostly inexperienced bag of Continental generals who faced armies of both Tories and British regulars. General Benjamin Lincoln of Massachusetts, along with a mixed force of militia and Continentals, marched south to support a French attack on a virtually defenseless Savannah, Georgia. The French admiral Comte d'Estaing demanded the surrender of the small British garrison in the name of Louis XVI. He then established an elaborate siege of the city, but on October 9 botched the entire attack, incurring 800 casualties. With that dubious accomplishment, and fearing bad weather, d'Estaing packed up his army and sailed away to Martinique, leaving Lincoln to wonder at the value of the French alliance. The American general marched his remaining troops back to Charleston, South Carolina, leaving Savannah in British hands.

General Lincoln did not possess Washington's survival skills and bottled up his army in Charleston. Clinton's 10,000 men closed in, while Tarleton sealed every escape road. When Lincoln finally surrendered on May 12, 1780, he was treated with complete disdain.

Meanwhile, General Horatio Gates brought an army south to attack Cornwallis, who had been building forts in the Carolinas. Gates's poor generalship was consistent. On August 16, he blundered into Cornwallis's superior force near Camden, North Carolina. Instead of a prudent withdrawal, Gates attacked. The resulting one-sided slaughter by the Tory Legion left Tarleton's men so exhausted they could hardly lift their swords to hack down fleeing rebels.

Gates's army of almost 3,000 troops had been slashed to a bedraggled band of 700 without food or equipment. American dead amounted to almost 2,000 men, whereas the British had lost only 69 soldiers. Clinton returned to New York, and Cornwallis achieved command in the south. Now Cornwallis decided to sweep northeast and build his Tory army. To this end he assigned Major Patrick Ferguson and about 1,000 Tories to secure his left flank.

ABOVE Banastre Tarleton (1754–1833) was considered to be the most hated officer in the British Army. His oppressive tactics offered little or no quarter to his enemies and he was willing to use any means necessary to achieve his goals.

"Buck and Ball" for Continental Muskets

In battles between British regulars and Continental troops, the standard weapon was the smoothbore musket. Usually, the hopelessly inaccurate long flintlocks were discharged en masse on command and reloaded as quickly as possible for the next volley. In 1777, however, George Washington authorized the use of one .69 caliber ball and three .31 caliber buckshot in each musket load to increase the power of every American volley. Called "Buck and Ball," the load was never used by the British or French.

Ferguson arrogantly warned the scattered bands of American trappers, hunters, and "over-the-mountain" men in today's Tennessee that they must join the Crown troops or be invaded. Ferguson sadly miscalculated. Soon, almost 900 hard-living, hard-drinking, sharp-shooting mountain-men were hunting Ferguson's Tory army. He stood his ground atop Kings Mountain, a long, narrow plateau-topped ridge.

Ferguson's Tories had been taught to fight like British regulars with Brown Bess muskets and bayonets. The mountain-men under Colonels Isaac Shelby and "Nolichucky Jack" Sevier were long-range riflemen who used knives and tomahawks for close work. Indian war whoops began the battle—on October 7, 1780—and the buckskin-clad warriors stormed the plateau from all sides. Firing as they climbed through dense woods, the long-riflemen aimed low and sheared away line after line of Tories, while musket volleys hissed high above the mountain-men's heads. Tory bayonet charges met no resistance. Soon the riflemen gained the top of Kings Mountain and the Tories began trying to surrender under rising and falling tomahawks. Unable to accept surrender, Ferguson wheeled his horse and charged with sword raised. He was shot to pieces by 50 rifles. The British concept of "fighting Americans with Americans" had failed miserably.

RIGHT An engraving depicting the British "Regulars" in their parade uniforms posed next to a British cavalryman, representing two of the finest European fighting forces.

Cowpens – Tarleton Shattered, Cornwallis Marches to Yorktown

1781

FACED WITH THE mounting threats in the south, George Washington brought in his best commanders. On December 2, 1780, Major General Nathanael Greene inherited survivors from the wretched Horatio Gates. Their paper strength was 2,500, but only 1,500 showed up for duty, and only 800 of those were equipped for the field. Greene moved the mob into a "camp of repose" 60 miles southeast of Charlotte, North Carolina. There, he and some very able officers began to whip them back into shape. Among these officers were Colonel John Eager Howard, Polish engineer Thadeusz Kosciuszko, the able cavalry commander William Washington, and—drawn from his 1779 retirement—the "Old Waggoner" Daniel Morgan. Crippled by arthritis and sciatica, he accepted the rank of Brigadier General and answered Washington's call to duty.

Greene divided his already small force into three commands. Each unit could strike at Cornwallis's communications outposts, ambush his supply lines, or harass his flanks. Whichever unit Cornwallis moved against, Greene could strike elsewhere. Puzzled by this information from Tory scouts on the divided command, Cornwallis picked up the challenge and divided his own command, attacking each of Greene's three groups. For good measure, he chose Banastre Tarleton with his Legion of dragoons, Highlanders, infantry, light artillery, and a group of Tories totalling 1,100 men to dispose of Morgan's "nuisance."

The towering, burly Morgan, clad in buckskins, chose his fighting ground with care; a sprawling cow pasture, known locally as "cowpens," with no trees to

ABOVE Four uniformed Continental Army "Regulars" in conversation, wearing the common blue coat faced with red, white, or buff, to distinguish State units. The officer (left) carries a "spontoon" spear and wears a short sword.

inhibit movement of troops or cavalry, but with hills and depressions perfect for concealment.

On January 16, as Tarleton's exhausted troops bedded down a short distance away after a killing march, Morgan visited every campfire to explain his plan and cheer his men.

Tarleton began his advance at 3.00 a.m. Tory scouts brought back news that militia had been sighted and that Morgan's main body was nearby. Tarleton was elated and spurred ahead with 50 dragoons. They spotted the usual ragged mob of militia, swung into line and trotted forward. Gunfire sheeted across the tall grass from Morgan's picked marksmen. Fifteen saddles emptied and Tarleton halted. He waved forward his infantry, who came at the double. The militia waited, and then a second aimed rifle volley shattered the sound of wailing Highland bagpipes. A dozen British officers and NCOs dropped. The militia ran to the rear

BROWN BESS MUSKET

The Short Land Service Musket used by the Regulars of the British infantry during the Revolutionary War had its barrel shortened to 42 inches from the clumsy 46-inch barrel of its predecessor. It weighed about 11 pounds without the 15-inch bayonet. Both muskets were called "Brown Bess," probably from the "browning" of the steel parts to prevent rust and the natural brown stock. The musket could hit a target five feet in diameter at 100 yards.

through a second line of riflemen.

Seeing only militia, Tarleton urged his dressed ranks forward. The second line fired at 50 paces. British soldiers toppled and recoiled. The first line had reloaded and added a volley that further bloodied the ground. Then all the militia ran, splitting left and right around a rising hill. With a collective roar, the enraged British infantry broke ranks and charged up the rise. Tarleton and his cavalry swept forward.

British troops surged over the crest and into the grim-faced ranks of Marylander and Delaware Continentals arrayed in von Steuben's parade-ground lines. Howard's first volley decimated the regulars. Tarleton's Legion galloped in to be hit on their flank by Colonel William Washington's dragoons and Lieutenant Colonel James McCall's sword-wielding cavalry. Virginia riflemen raked the other flank. Howard's final volley at point-blank range, followed by a bayonet charge into the bloody mass of Highlanders, finished it.

Abandoned by his Legion, Tarleton escaped, but he was broken that day. Cornwallis pursued Greene's army, but lost a race to the River Dan across which Greene escaped, ready to inflict further destruction on Cornwallis's line of communications. Cornwallis found himself holing up in a Virginia coastal village on the River James called Yorktown.

RIGHT Cavalry holsters for dragoon and other large single-shot pistols. They are designed to be belted around the horse's neck to avoid interfering with the cavalryman's sword or pike-work while mounted.

BELOW Colonel Tarleton's Dragoons are surprised by American cavalry commanded by Colonel William Washington. The British cavalry were sweeping down on retreating militia when Washington successfully counter-attacked.

French March with Washington to Yorktown

1781

By 1781, THE AMERICAN ARMY was, as Washington wrote, "at the end of our tether." Washington was convinced he could not defeat the British unless by some bold stroke of luck. Curiously, the British were coming to that same conclusion regarding their own chances of victory. The simple thrashing of some ranting rabble had turned into seven years of bloody campaigning and still the American army stood undefeated. It had been beaten and beaten, chased and beaten again, but refused to capitulate. Instead, the provincials had chastened several of Britain's finest general officers and had routed some of the finest regiments of foot and horse. And now the opportunistic French had come in with their equally opportunistic allies, the Dutch and Spanish, sniffing for plunder at Britain's expense. With the fleet stretched thin and British admirals seeing French sail stalking every possession and port in the empire, prolonging the North American adventure seemed to be a bad investment.

And yet Lieutenant General Lord Cornwallis saw a glimmer of hope. He had driven his army into Virginia, the heart of the Americans' economy and supply lines, and a center of radical resistance. Only the Marquis de Lafayette and Anthony Wayne had small forces in the field, and Cornwallis kept these at bay with what remained of the battered Lieutenant Colonel Banastre Tarleton's dragoons and through superior numbers of infantry and guns.

Over in New York, Lieutenant General Sir Henry Clinton ordered Cornwallis to select a headquarters on the Virginia coast. Cornwallis chose Yorktown, Virginia, which was set on a short spur of land flanked by the James and York rivers, with its back to Chesapeake Bay and the Atlantic Ocean beyond. There, he felt safe.

What Cornwallis did not know was that the French

DOCUMENTS

6. The Treaty of Alliance, signed in May 1778, brought France into Revolution on the United States' side. The French could now openly back the colonies with troops, ships, and weapons, where before they had been forced to aid the United States covertly. Burgoyne's defeat sealed the deal.

7. British General Cornwallis penned this letter to General George Washington on October 17, 1781, asking for a truce. Cornwallis had sent another letter to British General Clinton in New York, stating the impossible position of the Yorktown fortifications.

8. The Treaty of Paris, signed in 1783 ended all conflict between Great Britain and the United States, and introduced the former British colonies to the world as a free and independent country.

(see pocket page 31)

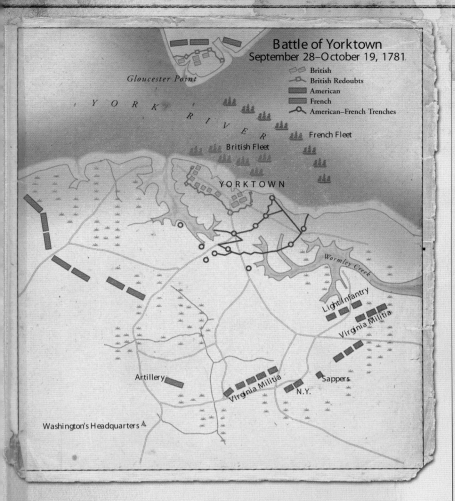

Battle of Yorktown
September 28–October 19, 1781

- ▭ British
- ⬠ British Redoubts
- ▬ American
- ▭ French
- ⌒ American–French Trenches

Gloucester Point

Y O R K   R I V E R

French Fleet

British Fleet

Y O R K T O W N

Wormley Creek

Light Infantry

Virginia Militia

Artillery

Virginia Militia

N.Y.

Sappers

Washington's Headquarters

were heading for Chesapeake Bay. When 3,000 French troops were landed on August 30 to swell Lafayette's command, and both Washington and Rochambeau arrived with their combined force, Cornwallis found his army of 7,800 facing 16,000 troops, artillery, and engineers, who were already busy snaking trenches through the sandy soil toward his redoubts. He must have looked longingly out to sea as the first artillery barrage fell on Yorktown.

French guns and the heavy guns of myopic but relentless Henry Knox hammered the British trench works and the town. Other faces were part of the encircling army who had stayed with the cause since Breed's and Bunker Hill in '75. In a bold sally, Captain Alexander Hamilton led his command in a rush that captured a key British redoubt. The sound of shovels filled the night as the allied trenches and guns moved closer. General Howe would have remembered: "Never give the rebels time to dig."

On September 5, Admiral de Grasse sortied out into the Virginia Capes and turned away an inferior force led by British Admiral Graves. With Clinton holed up in New York and every escape route closed, Cornwallis asked for a truce on October 17. Two days later, his army marched into captivity between silent ranks of American and French soldiers. Cornwallis sent his second in command, General O'Hara, to offer his sword. The British general offered the blade to Rochambeau, who declined, deferring to Washington. Putting on his best Virginia autocrat face, General George Washington directed O'Hara to present Cornwallis's sword of surrender to General Lincoln, who had been so badly treated by the British at Charlestown. Alongside the American officers, Lafayette remarked: "Sir, the dance is over."

General Comte de Rochambeau had marched his French troops from Rhode Island to link up with Washington's command. Nor did Cornwallis know French Admiral Comte de Grasse and a fleet of 28 sail

Unfinished Business – Strong Central Government or States' Rights?

THE UNITED STATES OF AMERICA began as an experiment in anarchy. The European world took a long look at the motley collection of states, each scrambling for itself in a confederation held together by a set of articles so limited in its power structure that each state virtually became a nation unto itself. The Comte de Vergennes, France's foreign minister and the United States' champion at Louis XVI's court, surveyed the tragic tangle that was America's postwar government and commented: "the American Confederation has a great tendency toward dissolution."

Each state legislature began testing the waters and either followed the Federalist lead of John Adams and New York's Alexander Hamilton, who preached for strong central government, or accepted Thomas Jefferson's Republican stand for strong states' rights. Using Thomas Paine's Common Sense and Jefferson's Declaration of Independence as models wherein troubles flowed from a tyrannical monarch and a corrupt central government, the Articles of Confederation stripped away most executive and central authority. Great Britain was convinced that the United States was impotent and falling apart. It sent no minister to New York where the Congress met, and John Adams, minister to Great Britain, received a cool, almost dismissive reception. In America, foreign ministers were required to present their portfolios to the governors of all 13 states. Trade tariffs between states hampered interstate commerce. Talking to the states about raising funds to pay debts and fix roads or ports

was, Robert Morris said, "like preaching to the dead." During a financial depression in Massachusetts, the state militia suppressed a taxpayers' revolt.

With virtually all the Founding Fathers out of the country, or back in their home states, only one veteran legislator and diplomat, John Jay, argued for abandoning sectional self-interest for a strong central government. James Madison seized on a Virginia convention organized to regulate commerce with Maryland to suggest a more encompassing purpose

ABOVE Benjamin Franklin is greeted in Philadelphia on September 14, 1785, by his daughter Sarah Bache, her family, and friends on his return from France after a stay of more than eight years.

involving all 13 states. Ultimately, with the blessing of Congress, 55 representatives from 12 states—Rhode Island boycotted—once more made their way to Philadelphia.

Among their number were Jefferson, abroad in Paris, and Adams, who was being ignored in the Court of St. James in London. George Washington was begged to attend by both Republicans and Federalists as a "presiding eminence." Into the mix of astounding intellect and folksy rumination came

Alexander Hamilton, sent by New York's Governor Clinton along with two anti-Federalist representatives to help curb his passion. They failed.

Hamilton was unique in that he owed allegiance to no state. He was born in Nevis, British West Indies on January 11, 1757. His birth parents were questionable, but his talent for learning was well documented and voracious. Working in a counting house, his intellect was so respected that his superiors raised his fare to sail to the American colonies and study law at Kings College in New York. The Revolution interrupted those studies, but placed him alongside his long-time benefactor, George Washington. His fortunes continued to rise until he arrived at the Constitutional Convention believing in a strong central government, a central bank and a strong army—which he one day hoped to lead; he loved uniforms.

Embracing the researches of another delegate, James Madison, Hamilton went to work on a series of essays touting the Federalist demands for a unified nation under a strong government with an elected leader, a legislature, and a judiciary. He signed these essays "Publius," and was joined in their writing by Madison and John Jay.

On September 14, 1785, 80-year-old Benjamin Franklin returned home after eight years in France. These delegates joined in debate to create a second revolution to govern the affairs of their countrymen.

DISBANDING THE ARMY

By 1783, the Continental army was disbanding, as armies in the field turned in their muskets, drums, and accoutrements. Units paraded for the last time, said their farewells and headed home. Congress had no money and farms needed planting. It was not until 1791 that Congress created a fulltime standing army - the Legion of the United States.

Madison and Hamilton Sell the Constitution to Congress

JAMES MADISON STOOD five feet four inches and weighed about 100 pounds. He had a high, bald forehead and wore only black to work. His voice was low, but his words carried to every seat in the convention. Born in Port Conway, Virginia on March 16, 1751, he was in his mid-thirties when he began lobbying for the Federalist cause at the constitutional convention in Philadelphia. He looked like a quiet mortician alongside his brutally outspoken colleague, the flashily dressed, redheaded ladies' man Alexander Hamilton.

The delegates met in the East Room of the State House where the Declaration of Independence had been signed, seated at tables where separate debates were held. Robert Morris suggested George Washington preside as president and that motion was unanimously approved. On May 25, 1787, the convention was gaveled to order.

Madison had their goals read under the subterfuge of "correcting the Articles of Confederation." What followed were 14 resolutions that chucked the Articles

into a cocked hat in favor of a central government with a National Legislative body that represented the states and headed by a National Executive with powers granted by Congress. These branches were watched over by a National Judiciary. What was read out to the assembly was the result of Madison's research into history's republics to that time and a sweeping appreciation of checks and balances needed to efficiently and fairly maintain the governing body.

The cards were on the table, formally polarizing the states into two parties, into agrarian tradition against industrial progress, and dividing the country into northern and southern sympathies and the balance of large states versus small. What Madison had proposed and Hamilton defended passed through committees of detail and style, and bitter debates over slavery and geography, suffrage and the power of the presidency, to arrive at a great compromise that satisfied no one but was approved by everyone in the hall that day, September 17, 1787.

After four months of debate and compromise, the delegates had decided to replace the Articles of

ABOVE LEFT Alexander Hamilton, writing under the name "Publius" wrote, along with Madison, a series of published essays laying out the need to ratify the new constitution. These essays - called the "Federalist Papers" - were critical factors in selling the new government model to the States.

LEFT James Madison was a small man with a huge intellect. No representative was more respected at the Constitutional Convention. He essentially conceived the Constitution, its stipulation of three governing branches and then worked with Alexander Hamilton to sell it to the assembled States' representatives.

Confederation with a more centralized United States Constitution. They adjourned and headed for the City Tavern. Selling it to the folks back home would be an even harder job.

One by one, in statehouse sessions filled with passion, oratory, slander, invective, the states finally ratified the document. When the deed was done, friends of the Constitution organized celebrations in major towns and state capitals. Following the jubilation in Philadelphia, patriot physician Benjamin Rush wrote to John Adams that, at last, the Constitution "…made us a nation."

In September 1789, at the first meeting of the new Congress, James Madison presented 10 amendments called The Bill of Rights (passed on September 25, 1789), which chiefly guaranteed individual rights, as well as freedom of speech and religion. Of the three branches of government—legislative, judicial, and executive—the executive had been the object of the most suspicion. However, an august presence had been among them throughout the process. Now, all heads turned toward the man who had kept the army together and hope alive during the Revolution. Following a popular election, George Washington was unanimously selected by the electoral college as the first president of the United States. He arrived in New York for his inauguration on April 30, 1789. With John Adams as vice president—he received the second-largest number of votes—and a Congress made up of some of the most brilliant minds of the era, the American government became as much explorers as those pioneers who were crossing the Appalachian Mountains to see what was on the other side.

LEFT George Washington's gold-headed walking can. He carried this stick through his civilian life and presidency. Tall, elegant, and serene, he was an ideal choice as President of the Constitutional Convention.

Jefferson Looks for Elbow Room

THOMAS JEFFERSON.
Third President of the United States

1795

DURING THE TUMULTUOUS TIMES the United States experienced under the government of the Articles of Confederation, Spain was the largest landholder in North America. The King of Spain owned Florida, coastal land in Alabama, Mississippi, the banks of the River Mississippi from Natchez to the Gulf of Mexico, and everything south of Canada and west of that river. East of the river, many of the states planned to turn the waterway—open or closed to navigation—to their financial gain.

But by the time the Americans had created their Constitution, the French were lopping off the heads of government in the Revolution of 1789. Also at this time, a certain young French officer of Corsican birth told his fellow officers that: "Revolutions are ideal times for soldiers with a bit of wit and the courage to act."

Soon, the new French Republic had declared war on Britain and Spain. This war split American sympathies, but being non-combatants, their primary interest was how to avoid damage and somehow come out ahead. This the United States managed with the Treaty of San Lorenzo, signed on October 27, 1795. The border with Spanish Florida was fixed at the 31st parallel and the River Mississippi was opened for American trade to the Gulf of Mexico and beyond.

John Adams became president in 1796 and walked a tightrope to avoid a war with France. By the turn of his term, the French had negotiated Louisiana from Spain and American relations with France had deteriorated. That Corsican officer—Napoleon Bonaparte—needed cash. President Thomas Jefferson, former minister to France James Monroe, and the current resident French minister, Robert R. Livingston, offered to accommodate Napoleon; Jefferson strongly hinted that the United States Congress was ready to side with Britain against the French. Napoleon did not need another adversary.

On July 14, 1803, a courier handed President Jefferson an envelope containing the Louisiana Purchase, which had been signed on April 30, together with Livingston's and Monroe's cover letter. The letter noted, apologetically, that they had managed "an acquisition of so great an extent [that] was, we well know, not contemplated by our appointment." For $15 million that "acquisition" amounted to over 529

ABOVE President Thomas Jefferson, illegally and secretly purchased the Louisiana Territory from France and went to Congress with a *fait accompli*. Fortunately, Congress saw his wisdom and authorized payment of the bill.

LEFT The signing of the Treaty of Mortefontaine between Napoleon Bonaparte and the United States which enabled the sale of Louisiana to America.

RIGHT Bridal Veil Falls, tumbling 620 feet down the canyon walls of what became Yosemite National Park in the Sierra Nevada mountains, was one of the wonders westward travelers discovered as they followed the footsteps of Lewis and Clark.

DOCUMENTS

14. The Louisiana Purchase, drafted by the French government and signed by Napoleon Bonaparte, ceded over 500 million acres of ground west of the Mississippi River to the United States at a cost of about three cents an acre.

15. President Thomas Jefferson wrote this letter to his then secretary, Meriwether Lewis, requesting that Lewis take charge of creating the "Corps of Discovery" and lead a party of explorers west to follow the Missouri River to – if possible – the Pacific Ocean.

(see pocket page 55)

Virginian Meriwether Lewis (1774–1809), the son of a wealthy father, had an adventurous disposition. In 1794, he volunteered with the troops who put down the Whiskey Rebellion in western Pennsylvania. His natural curiosity led him west where he learned Indian languages and woodcraft. A neighbor of Thomas Jefferson, he became the President's personal secretary and was invited to explore the territory of the Louisiana Purchase. Following that triumph, he became moody and withdrawn, dying from a self-inflicted pistol shot in a tavern near Nashville, Tennessee.

Meriwether Lewis

million acres—at three cents an acre—of western land. Curiously, Napoleon sold what he did not yet own, responding to Jefferson's roll of the dice. In brokering the acquisition, Jefferson wrote, he had "stretched the Constitution until it cracked."

The American odyssey was turning west and this purchase threw open the gates. On January 18, 1803, three months before the purchase was signed, President Jefferson sent a secret letter to Congress asking for $2,500 to fund an expedition that would cross the River Mississippi, head west and keep going. "The interests of commerce," he wrote, "place the principal object within the constitutional powers and care of Congress. That it should incidentally advance the geographic knowledge of our own continent," he added, "can not but be an additional gratification."

Lieutenant Meriwether Lewis, naturalist, Indian fighter with a knowledge of their languages, and in 1801 Jefferson's private secretary, had begun extensive preparation with known travelers' accounts and maps of Louisiana. Meticulously, Lewis planned a two-year journey into the uncharted west. He called upon an army friend, William Clark, to accompany him and the "Corps of Discovery." Clark was a brilliant choice. An engineer with knowledge of topography and surveying, he also knew and respected many of the Indian tribes they would encounter. As Lewis and Clark prepared to move out, other Americans loaded wagons, hitched up their oxen, and added their number to the great westward migration.

Jefferson Goes to War Against the Barbary Pirates

1804

MANY THINGS HAD BEEN ON Thomas Jefferson's mind when he walked the two blocks from his boarding house to the Capitol building on March 4, 1801. First off, his legs itched. He was the first president to be sworn in wearing long pants, instead of knee britches. Next, after taking the oath of office he wanted to heal the wounds of the election, the personal attacks, and harsh invective. And finally, there were the Barbary pirates.

Since the end of the Revolution in 1783, American shipping in the Mediterranean had been victimized by pirates. Using long galleys powered by oars and lateen sails, the corsairs staged their raids from bays and coves along the shores of Morocco, Algeria, Tunisia, and Tripolitania. Armed with swivel guns mounted fore and aft, they cowed unarmed merchant vessels and steered sailors and cargo into captivity to be sold as slaves or ransomed. To avoid these attacks, countries that were already involved in conflicts elsewhere found it easier to pay tribute to the Mediterranean pashas who controlled the pirates.

By 1803, the United States navy had a squadron of six heavy frigates. The idea of paying tribute to Pasha Yusuf Karamanli of Tripolitania raised the hackles of President Jefferson, Secretary of State James Madison, and Secretary of War Henry Dearborn. By the time Jefferson was sworn in, the United States had paid over $2 million to the pirates' masters. The President was determined to try all avenues of negotiation, but that ground had been trod before with no success.

Meanwhile, the sloop Enterprise was returning from Malta when a Barbary corsair, the Tripoli, appeared hull up on the horizon. Flying a British ensign to draw the pirate closer, Lieutenant Andrew Sterrett waited until the corsair captain, Admiral Rais Mahomet Rous, called across that he was hunting Americans.

Sterrett ran up the Stars and Stripes and opened fire. American gunnery tore into the 14-gun warship. When Rais tried to grapple, US marines swept the deck with musket fire. Rais lowered his colors in surrender, but when Sterrett moved in to accept, the admiral raised them again and fired. Sterrett pounded the pirate ship into a sinking wreck, killed most of the crew, and left Rais bobbing in the sea beneath a jury-rigged mast. When the defeated admiral arrived in front of the Pasha, the humiliated monarch sent the wretched Rais through the streets of Tripoli riding backwards

on a jackass with sheep entrails wrapped around his neck, and later awarded him 500 lashes on the soles of his feet.

With diplomacy exhausted, Jefferson sent Commodore Edward Preble to Tripoli with a squadron of American warships. During the maneuvering, the frigate Philadelphia ran aground. It was towed away by the Pasha's sailors and its crew imprisoned for a $200,000 ransom. The answer was a daring raid by Lieutenant Stephen Decatur on the night of February 16, 1804, during which the captured frigate was burnt to the waterline. Preble's squadron then began a crashing bombardment of Tripoli.

As the guns continued to roar, the United States launched land and sea attacks, including an assault by US marines leading a polyglot force of mercenaries, who seized the harbor fortress of Derna on April 25, 1805. With the US navy kicking at his front door and marines swarming from the desert at his back, the Pasha reached for his pen. On June 4, 1805, he signed a treaty in the main cabin of the frigate Constitution. Following the war of 1812 and the Napoleonic War in 1815, the Barbary pirate threat ended completely from "the shores of Tripoli."

ABOVE William Bainbridge, captain of the frigate George Washington, and later the Philadelphia, delivers tribute money from the United States to the Dey of Algiers in 1800. He was later imprisoned with his crew.

LEFT A swivel gun, commonly used to threaten smaller ships or subdue any resistance, when loaded with grape shot. Marines usually manned the swivel guns in ship-to-ship confrontations.

Pirate Galley

The pirates of the Barbary Coast employed slender oar-powered galleys rowed by slaves, which easily closed on merchant ships that relied on the soft breezes crossing the Mediterranean Sea. Armament consisted of swivel guns mounted along the sides and one or two big guns in the bows. But their chief weapon was the crew, often numbering 100 or more, armed with curved swords, pistols, and muskets, who swarmed aboard their victims' ships.

BELOW Though he is shown here in dire straits, Stephen Decatur's actions against the Barbary pirates were successful. As the American Navy wrecked the pirates' galleys, the United States Marines captured Derna on the shores of Tripoli.

Honor, Politics, and Hamilton's Farewell

1804

THE YEAR 1804 was one of gain and loss for the United States. On May 30, 1804, Captain Meriwether Lewis, Captain William Clark, and a collection of rugged adventurers calling themselves the Corps of Discovery began the exploration of the territories of the new Louisiana Purchase. President Jefferson's stroke of luck and statesmanship had exploded the country's western boundary almost to the Pacific Ocean. At the stroke of a pen the United States had doubled in size and this success had become the Republican hammer that drove another nail into the Federalist coffin.

The nation's leading Federalist Alexander Hamilton, who along with James Madison had ramrodded the Constitution through Congress, slipped into a deep depression. Jefferson's second term was assured and Hamilton would be once again on the sidelines. He was building a house, "The Grange" in northern Manhattan, as well as practicing law in the New York courts.

Another prominent individual had also been marginalized as Jefferson cut loose Aaron Burr as his vice president in favor of George Clinton, the recently elected governor of New York. Burr had dallied with secessionists while in office and his naked ambition, evident to everyone who knew him, eventually led to his downfall. In their depressed states both Burr and Hamilton were vulnerable to the usual gossip and political butchery that prattled on in most social events. Word reached Burr that Hamilton had been extremely indiscreet in his commentary and Burr sent off a note requesting explanation or retraction or both.

Hamilton, as head of the Society of Cincinnati, an organization of Revolutionary War officers, stood fast

ABOVE Lawyer, soldier, politican, author, first U.S. Treasurer, Hamilton's life had been full in the service of his country. Only his personal ambition, ego and ability to make enemies tarnished his career and then ended it.

LEFT Aaron Burr fires a fatal bullet that cut down Alexander Hamilton and lodged next to his spine. The two men were both brilliant, but also flawed by their arrogance and ambition. Burr eventually died a ruined man.

and refused a retraction that would have "rendered me unworthy of your esteem," he wrote to his wife. Burr's personal antagonism erupted in an exchange of letters so insulting that only a duel could save each man's "honor."

The ritual of the duel was fixed in that each man communicated through "seconds"—designated friends or colleagues—up to the time of the "interview," as the actual face-to-face shooting was called. Hamilton had been awarded delays to put his affairs in order. On occasion, he remarked to friends his willingness to waste his shot. Burr, on the other hand, being the initially wronged party, was far more sanguine. The wood of Weehawken on the Hudson River was chosen and both parties were rowed to the spot as the morning haze burned off the river. Doctor David Hosack, a physician, remained with the boatmen clear of the field should he be needed.

A boxed set of identical .54-caliber dueling pistols with nine-inch barrels were presented. Each used modern percussion cap ignition and had manually-set hair triggers. Hamilton declined to have his pistol's trigger set for a light pull. In their shirtsleeves, the pair were led to an open field. They cocked their weapons and each paced off ten paces—about 20 feet. Standing in the dew-wet grass, Burr and Hamilton faced each other. At the command "present," both pistols came up. The blasts erupted between them. Hamilton's shot went wide, nicking the branch off a nearby tree. Burr's shot plowed into Hamilton's stomach piercing his liver, and lodging in his splintered vertebra against the spine. He toppled over and Nathaniel Pendleton, his second, ran forward to cradle him in his arms. Burr was hustled off the field just before the doctor made his way up from the river.

Burr was indicted for murder and fled. His reputation shattered, he lived in obscurity until his death in 1836. Alexander Hamilton with his brilliant intellect flawed by vanity lingered for 30 hours and died in excruciating pain on July 12, 1804— a soldier's death.

ABOVE Rising to Vice President of the United States, Burr was a shrewd politician driven by ambition and unbending pride. He served both himself and his country, but his duel with Hamilton destroyed his brilliant promise.

WEAPONS OF THE DUEL

Though swords were as fashionable among eastern gentlemen as were knives down south (used in fights with the wrists tied together), pistols were the American duelist's most common weapon. One of the wronged parties would provide the single shot pistols, often in an elegantly boxed set. Seconds loaded the pistols with great care under strict observation. Shots were fired any time after the command to fire. Distances between duelists varied between 10 and 20 paces.

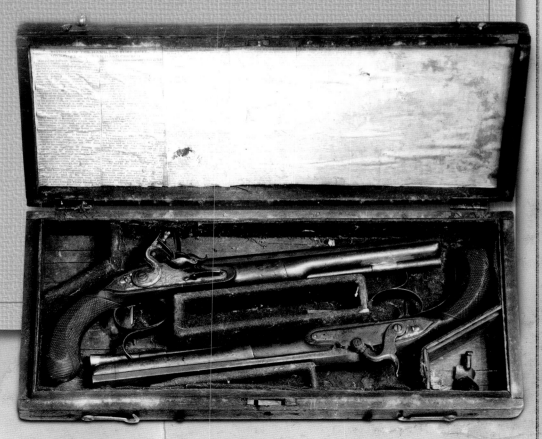

"Mr. Madison's War" is Declared

1812

THOUGH HE WAS OFTEN introduced to gatherings as the "Father of the Constitution"—a title he always disclaimed—people in the street and friends referred to James Madison as "Jimmy," or "Little Jim." He could not have been more different from the man he followed into the president's office, Thomas Jefferson, who often answered the White House door himself in bathrobe and bedroom slippers. Garbed in funereal black accenting his scarce white hair and high forehead, Madison was all energy and business. He inherited a country that was down at the heels, but brimming with ambition in every quarter of its polyglot population.

One other inheritance Madison received from Jefferson was that the United States was still at war with Great Britain, 29 years after the Treaty of Paris had ended the Revolution. The British in Canada wanted to keep their forts and trading posts around the Great Lakes to gather in the valuable fur trade they had established with the Indian tribes. They encouraged the Indians to attack the settlers who were pouring into Kentucky, Ohio, and the Illinois Territory. At sea, American ships were turned away from trading with British colonies and had to slip into obscure ports to evade these trade laws. This trade friction had earlier been aggravated by the declaration of war between France and Britain in 1793. France was the principal trade partner of the United States and more than 250 American ships were confiscated by British warships for carrying contraband. For 10 years, American diplomats, spurred by an outraged public and government, sought redress, compromise, or anything to ease the situation. When Napoleon heated up the war again in 1802, Britain began to press American sailors to fill the 150,000-man Royal Navy. "Once an Englishman, always an Englishman!" was the press-gang's cry.

President Jefferson wanted nothing to do with war. After fending off the war "hawks" in Congress for two terms, he headed home to Monticello, Virginia,

and left the problems to former secretary of state James Madison, America's fourth president.

Britain kept up pressure on the Indians throughout the frontier, and settlers were terrified. Finally, in November 1811, Indiana Territory Governor William Henry Harrison managed to pull together 900 American troops for a raid on a large village at Tippecanoe, which was commanded by Shawnee Chief Tecumseh's brother, the prophet Tenskwatawa. The American troops triumphed and, buoyed up

ABOVE Ships of the British fleet are shown bombarding Washington and sailing up the Potomac River as troops are landed for the march inland. Government buildings were put to the torch on August 24, 1814.

LEFT This view shows the east front of the President's House in Washington D.C. in 1807. The north and south porticos have been added. In 1814, British soldiers marched in and ate the dinner that had been prepared for President Madison.

Dolley Payne Todd Madison (1768–1840) became one of the most famous "first ladies" in United States history. The wife of President James Madison, she was the social heart of his administration. Her graces helped smooth over disagreements between statesmen, and she welcomed visitors from Indian chiefs to envoys. She had a keen political sense prized by her husband, and managed to save Washington's full-length portrait just ahead of the British before they burned the White House in 1812.

Dolley Madison

by this victory, Congress urged Madison to give the British a final warning. The President fired off a demand for the elimination of trade restrictions on American ships. In truth, an American embargo on British trade was working. British merchants had realized they needed American trade, but the slow response of Parliament to Madison's ultimatum prompted a divided, partisan Congress to vote for war on Great Britain.

The United States was unprepared and had no plan and no strategy except the punishment of Canada. The American army was small, poorly trained, under-funded, and led by elderly generals out of touch with field command. The navy consisted of just 16 warships. Troops were rushed up toward American Fort Detroit to intimidate the British and Canadians into abandoning their ships and surrendering. But the unprepared army fell apart during the march and plans for their attack fell into British hands. The attack was a debacle. Next, in trying to evacuate Fort Dearborn before the Indians arrived, American Captain William Wells arrived late. He charged forward toward the swarm of Indians and, in a masterpiece of questionable judgment, began cursing the Indian chiefs. They shot him out of the saddle and ate his heart raw. So began the War of 1812.

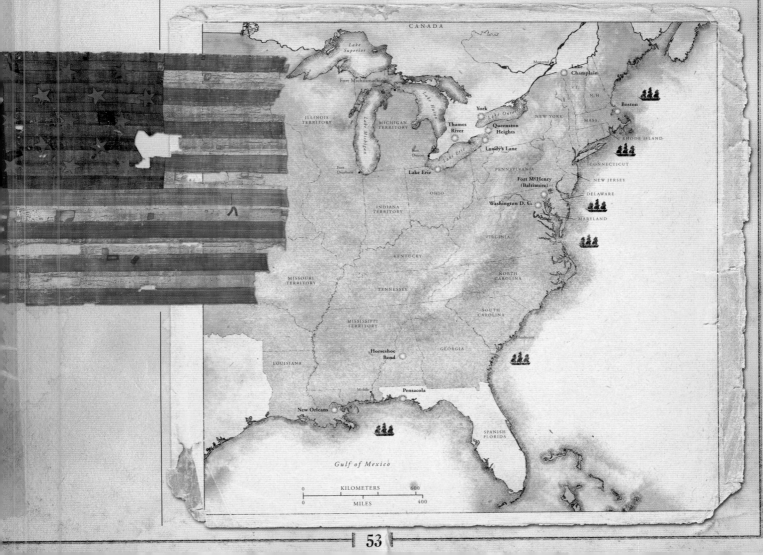

Madison's "Warhawks" on the Attack and on the Run

1814

FOR THE MOST PART, the land battles in the poorly planned invasion of Canada constituted one American disaster after another. No sooner had Fort Detroit and Fort Dearborn fallen than the public, Congress, and President Madison demanded new generals and victories. Tecumseh's attempt to unite the Indians now drew previously reluctant tribes—Creek, Delaware, Cherokee, and Kickapoos—to attack frontier settlers. Ambushes and massacres enraged the public back east, who had been expecting quick victories up north.

James Madison did his best as a wartime president. He made it a point to personally visit every department of the army and navy to whip up enthusiasm. He offset his funereal suit by wearing a small round hat topped by an enormous cockade. He was everywhere reviewing troops before they marched off to battle.

William Henry Harrison, the hero of Tippecanoe, raised an army of keen-eyed woodsmen from Kentucky and Tennessee, and headed north to retake Fort Detroit. Patriotic zeal was dampened by torrential rains, swollen rivers, and impassable trails. He camped to wait for winter when frozen ground would be the Americans' ally. Meanwhile, British General Sir Isaac Brock with 1,600 troops and 300 Indians was seeking to defend against the crossing of the Niagara River by 6,000 American troops under General Stephen van Rensselaer. The inexperienced van Rensselaer divided his troops and on October 13 sent 800 troops across under the command of Lieutenant Colonel Winfield Scott, having given orders for the rest of his army to cross

downstream. This they failed to do and sat on the opposite bank while Scott's party was shot up and captured. Unfortunately for the British, General Brock was killed, removing the best field commander they had.

Up at Lake Champlain, General Henry Dearborn's attack with 6,000 troops against Montreal on November 19, 1812, ran into trouble against the 1,900 British Canadian defenders. As the battlefield grew dark, the British troops withdrew, but the Americans pressed on. Dearborn's units became separated and soon began shooting at each other. Eventually, the general's army refused to go on and many of his troops packed up and went home because their enlistments had come to an end. Everywhere, what its critics called "Mr. Madison's War" was a disaster.

By 1814, the British had prepared a three-pronged invasion, which would eventually target New York, Washington, Baltimore, and New Orleans in the Deep South. Their orders from Admiral Alexander Cochrane were to burn, sack, and pillage as payback for American tactics in the north. After entering Chesapeake Bay on August 14, and driving off gunboat defenses, General Robert Ross marched his troops into the nation's capital and put the city to the torch. The President's evacuation party received word of the raid's success at a tavern in Montgomery Courthouse, Maryland. President Madison's wife, Dolley, barely got out of the residence before British troops arrived to find the evening dinner still warm on the table. They ate, and then burned the President's house down.

By September 11, the British fleet was arrayed against

Baltimore's Fort McHenry. Kept at a distance by sunken blockade ships, the cannonade rained over 1,800 solid shot and shells into the fort. Rockets were fired to show gunners their targets. Standing at the rail of a ship in the harbor, Francis Scott Key scratched the lines of a poem that ended when he saw the American Star-Spangled Banner still flying from the fort's rampart after the 25-hour bombardment. Cochrane withdrew his ships. The New York attack had stalled, so all that remained of the invasion plan was the thrust at New Orleans, a prize whose loss would make the Yankees squirm.

A British Sailor's Life

━━⬥◆⬥━━

Life in the Royal Navy was brutal. During war, press gangs roamed England dragging off farmers, laborers, drunks, and petty criminals to sea in exchange for "the King's shilling." Sailors learned by doing, spurred on with kicks and floggings for offenses. Food was fair at the start of a voyage and grew worse as scurvy wracked the crew after the fruit and vegetables were gone. Battle deaths and loss of limbs required frequent replacement of crews. American sailors were frequent targets for the press gangs.

━━⬥◆⬥━━

The War at Sea and Improbable Victory

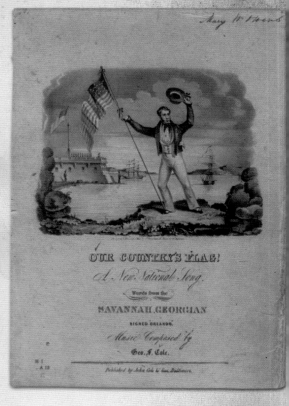

1815

BY THE END OF 1814, James Madison was desperate. What had started as a war to punish Great Britain had become a war of self-defense against British military might. The President's international diplomacy had failed. The army had failed. The country's fate was in the hands of a very few brave men.

The large American frigate Constitution out-sailed the smaller British frigate Guerrière captained by James Dacres, yet Dacres had demanded this showdown. The ships circled each other, maneuvering to gain the favorable wind, the gunner's advantage. Captain Isaac Hull, the Constitution's skipper, held his fire. Dacres had challenged any of the "inferior" American navy ships to meet him. Though rated as a frigate, the Constitution was 50 feet longer, had a wider beam, and mounted 50 iron guns, 24-pounders thrust through the gun-deck ports and 32-pound carronades lining the upper deck. Gun captains squinted along their barrels.

"Now, boys! Pour it into them!" screamed Hull as the Guerrière tried desperately to shear off. The 24-pounders fired as they bore, tearing up rigging, splintering wood, shattering taff rails, and blasting ratlines and hammock nettings to shreds. The 18-pound shot of the Guerrière bounced off the Constitution's white oak strakes buttressed by live oak frames. With a tortured crack, the Guerrière's mizzen mast splintered, hung in the jumble of its ruined rigging, and then sagged over the side. Hull made his turn across the Guerrière's bow, firing as he did so, and closed to 50 feet. The Constitution's short carronades hammered their 32-pound balls into the tangle of up-ended guns, sprawled bodies, and fallen yard-arms.

ABOVE "A new national song" claims the cover of this sheet music for "Our Country's Flag", an early title for what became "The Star Spangled Banner" tak form the poem by Francis Scott Key.

BELOW The frigate Constitution. (right closes in on the HMS Guerrière to begin a historic duel. British balls bounced off "Old Ironsides" and the American ship dismasted her British opponent.

Two hours after the contest began, Guerrière was holed to the waterline and dismasted. Dacres hauled down his colors and at 3.15 p.m., August 20, 1812, the British frigate Guerrière "sank out of sight."

On land, the American army was being badly led into appalling debacles, while at sea a new generation of brash young captains with their 38- and 50-gun frigates were winning battle after battle. The British frigates Frolic, Macedonian, and Java all fell to American guns. On the Great Lakes, Oliver Hazard Perry built a fleet of gunboats and frigates. On September 10, 1813, after breaking a blockade by hand-hauling his ships across a sandbar, Perry sailed his Lake Erie fleet straight at the British. After a furious battle that saw Perry move his flag from a sinking wreck to another ship, the apparently victorious British fleet was stunned when he attacked yet again. Holed, raked, and sinking, the British ships surrendered.

The final act of the War of 1812 was played out on January 8, 1815, across a swampy Louisiana field. General Andrew Jackson looked down his lines behind redoubts made of cotton bales. His troops were Creoles, Tennessee sharpshooters, free Blacks, local militia, Cajuns, and pirates. The British had been told these "dirty shirts" were cowards. With a roll of drums and the skirl of bagpipes, the troops advanced through the morning mist on Jackson's position. An American cannon filled with scrap-iron ripped out and killed 200 at a stroke. Jackson's riflemen, four rows deep, fired and fired and fired. Line after line of British infantry fell. The drums pounded, rifles crashed, bayonets flashed, and men died. The few surviving British soldiers were allowed to trudge back to their ships with their wounded.

No one on that field knew that on Christmas Eve, 1814, American and British delegations had met in Ghent, Belgium, and signed a treaty ending the war. Neither country won. Both countries lost part of a generation of brave young men. Great Britain and the United States never went to war again

A firebrand, Jackson (1767–1845) prospered in business and politics regardless of his short fuse and willingness to defend his "honor" against all comers. A man who had slandered his wife was killed by Jackson in a duel. He was the first resident of Tennessee to be elected to the House of Representatives and rose briefly to a seat in the Senate. Expecting the British to land troops near New Orleans, he used his personality, reputation, and old friendships to pull together a motley army that won the day. He was President from 1829 to 1837.

Major General Andrew Jackson
"Old Hickory"

The Founding
& the Future

THE FOUNDING FATHERS had seen the country take shape from its rustic roots to its western expansion and the dawn of industrialization. They had been at the helm during three wars—each conflict a near thing—and had conceived a government that has stood the test of time. They left behind problems that would fall to their heirs: slavery, national finances, Manifest Destiny, international trade, and the Native American population. But they also left us examples to draw upon for the solution of those issues. They were men flawed with vanity, impatience, and ambition. Yet the six men profiled here managed at key moments to rise above their flaws and place the needs of the people ahead of everything.

They acclimated slowly. The concept of being an "American" first and a Virginian, Pennsylvanian, North Carolinian, or New Yorker second was still a difficult fit, because local customs and local loyalties bound people together, regardless of what some papers and politicians might say. The United States was a nation of farmers, merchants, tradesmen, artisans, and men of letters in science, philosophy, the healing arts, and clergy who came from all levels of society. But now, with their own ground—twice won—beneath their feet, these Americans began to realize that, given the tools, they had the ability to rise to any level they sought.

During the first 50 years that followed that earliest cry for liberty, the Founding Fathers created the tools to lead men, write laws, and guarantee that liberty for future generations. The American people were

LEFT The romantic image of the trailblazing adventurer of the early nineteenth century was only partly true. Life was hard on the prairie or in the mountains and the basic tools of defense, medicine, and nutrition left a lot to be desired.

PUBLISHED BY CURRIER & IVES

Copyright 1876 by Currier & Ives, N.Y.

125 NASSAU ST. NEW YORK

THE PROGRESS OF THE CENTURY.

THE LIGHTNING STEAM PRESS.   THE ELECTRIC TELEGRAPH.   THE LOCOMOTIVE.   THE STEAMBOAT.

then able to address the huge and complex infrastructure of roads, rivers, canals, bridges, and ports along 1,000 miles of seacoast. They still relied on slaves for cheap farm labor. Their manufacturing capability was in its infancy and the merchant fleet was small by any standard. But this state of affairs had been predictable. As Benjamin Franklin wrote in the Pennsylvania Gazette on August 24, 1749: "In the settling of new countries, the first care of the planters must be to provide and secure the necessities of life; this engrosses their attention and affords them little time to think of anything farther. … Agriculture and mechanical arts were of the most immediate importance; the culture of minds by the finer arts and sciences was necessarily postponed to times of more wealth and leisure."

That time was now upon Americans and they seized its significance. Eli Whitney's cotton gin, patented in 1794, automated the process of cleaning cotton and created a booming cash crop for the southern states. His American system of interchangeable parts for rifle manufacture sparked the idea of mass production and helped launch American industry. On August 10, 1807, Robert Fulton's steamboat Clermont chugged from New York City to Albany, taking 32 hours to travel 150 miles at an average speed of about 5 miles per hour. Twenty-six years later, the John Bull steam locomotive rolled down the rails of the Camden & Amboy Railroad—the first in New Jersey. That year, 1833, saw the first of America's fleet of clipper ships racing across the seas beneath clouds of sail. Immigrant wagons rutted trails to the west, crossed the Mississippi and followed the rivers into lands where Native Americans had roamed for generations.

One by one, the great minds that created the structure where these ideas and concepts could flourish winked out. Adams and Jefferson died within two hours of each other on July 4, 1826—50 years to the day since the Declaration of Independence. When Madison was gone in 1836 all that remained was hewn in stone, modelled in paint, or written on paper in countenances and words that every American schoolchild knows.

Index

Credits

The authors wish to acknowledge the contributions of the following people who went the extra mile helping us accumulate the immense amount of research required for this book:

Marc Honorof, First Person Productions; Joan Bachrach, National Park Service (Valley Forge pictures); Jude Pfister, Morristown National Park Archives; Bill Tropeman, Valley Forge National Park Service; Scott Hauting, Valley Forge Archives; Michelle Ortwein, Valley Forge National Park Service; Yvonne Brooks, Library of Congress; Dolly Pantelides' U. S. Naval Academy Museum; Nick Crawford—The Granger Collection, and all those at Carlton.

PHOTOGRAPH CREDITS

The Publishers would like to thank the following sources for thier kind permission to reproduce agency and archive photographs in this book. Photograph location indicator: t-top, b-bottom, c-centre, l-left, r-right. Numbers are page numbers. nless otherwise noted, all original photography is by the author, Gerry Souter.

Library of Congress: 8 (c), (br); 10 (tr); 11 (tr); 12 (bc); 14 (b); 15 (b); 16 (bc); 18 (tr), (br); 19 (t); 20 (tr), (br); 23 (c); 24 (tr); 25 (cr), (b); 26 (tr), (b); 27 (tl), (br); 28 (tr); 30 (c); 31 (tr); 32 (tr), (bl); 33 (tl), (br); 34 (t), (b); 35 (b); 41 (b); 42 (c); 43 (tl), (cr), (b); 44 (tl), (tr); 45 (t); 50 (tr); 52 (tr), (br); 54 (tr), (b); 55 (tr), (br); 56 (tr); 57 (t), (bl); 58 (b); 59 (t), (cl), (cr); **National Park Service Archives:** 8 (tr); 15 (t); 16-17 (c); 19 (bl); 22-23 (tc); 28 (c); 29 (tl), (tr), (bl); 31 (cr); 33 (cl); 35 (tr); 36 (bl), (br); 39 (tc); 45 (br); 47 (tr); **The Granger Collection:** 9 (b); 10 (cl); 11 (b); 16 (tr); 17 (bc); 20 (c); 21 (br); 22 (br); 36 (tr); 37 (br); 38 (cl); 39 (b); 46 (tr); 47 (l); 48 (tr); 49 (cl), (b); 50 (b); 51 (tl); 52 (c); 53 (tr); 55 (cl). **Art Library International:** 11 (tl); 25 (tl); **Albany Institute of History and Art:** 12 (tl); 13 (b); **Fort Ticonderoga Historical Museum:** 17 (t); 48 (br); **College of Physicians of Philadelphia:** 23 (bl), (br); **New York Public Library:** 31 (bl); **Apple River Fort, Elizabeth, Illinois:** 38 (l); **Museum of the City of New York:** 40 (tr); **Collection of the Commonwealth of Virginia, Library of Virginia:** 40 (b); **The Bridgeman Art Library/Bibliotheque Nationale, Paris, France/Archives Charmet:** 46 (b); **Milwaukee Public Museum:** 51 (br); **Smithsonian Institution:** 53 (cl); **U.S. Naval Academy Archive:** 56 (b)

MEMORABILIA CREDITS

page 17 The Virginia Resolves, National Archives and Records Administration; **page 17** Declaration of Independenc—First draft, National Archives and Records Administration; **page 21** The final "Engrossed" Declaration, National Archives and Records Administration; **page 19** Continental Army Oath of Allegiance, National Archives and Records Administration; **page 22** Hand-drawn map of "Prince town," The Granger Collection; **page 38** Treaty of Alliance, National Archives and Records Administration; **page 38** Cornwallis' Letter to Washington, The Morgan Library; **page 38** Treaty of Paris, National Archives and Records Administration; **page 41** Articles of Confederation, National Archives and Records Administration; **page 43** The Constitution of the United States, National Archives and Records Administration; **page 43** The Federalist Papers, National Archives and Records Administration; **page 43** *The Bill of Rights*, National Archives and Records Administration; **page 43** Washington's Inaugural Address, National Archives and Records Administration; **page 44** The Louisiana Purchase, National Archives and Records Administration; **page 44** Jefferson's letter to Meriwether Lewis, National Archives and Records Administration.

BIBLIOGRAPHY

Paul F. Boller Jr., *Presidential Anecdotes*, Oxford University Press, New York, 1981

J.C.A. Stagg, *Mr. Madison's War*, Princeton University Press, New Jersey, 1983

Peter Hannaford, *The Essential George Washington*, Images From the Past, Inc., Bennington, Vermont, 1999

T. J. Stiles, *Founding fathers – In Their Own Words*, Pennsylvania State University, Perigee Book, New York, 1999

Howard F. Bremer, *John Adams – 1735-1826*, Oceana Publications, Dobbs Ferry, NY 1967

Gore Vidal, *Inventing a Nation*, Yale University Press, New Haven, 2003

Claude G. Bowers, *Jefferson and Hamilton*, Houghton Mifflin Company, Boston, 1966

Richard Wheeler, *Voices of 1776*, Thomas Crowell Company, New York, 1972

David McCullough, *1776*, Simon & Schuster, New York, 2005

Richard Brookhiser, *Alexander Hamilton – American*, The Free Press, New York, 1999

Charles Cerami, *Young Patriots*, Sourcebooks, Inc., Naperville, Illinois, 2005

Richard B. Morris, *The Forging of the Union – 1781-1789*, Harper & Row Publishers, New York, 1987

Charles A. Cerami, *Jefferson's Great Gamble*, Sourcebooks, Inc., Naperville, Illinois, 2003

PUBLISHING CREDITS

Editorial Director: Piers Murray Hill
Executive Editor: Gemma Maclagan
Design: Stefan Morris
Additional Design: Drew McGovern, Russell Knowles, Katie Baxendale and Chris Gould
Maps: Martin Brown
Copy Editor: Catherine Rubinstein
Picture research: Gerry Souter
Memorabilia research: Gerry Souter
Production: Lisa Cook